MEDITATIONS

By Marcus Aurelius

MARCUS AURELIUS ANTONINUS THE ROMAN EMPEROR

Table of Contents

Biography Of Marcus Aurelius 1
Introduction 10
The First Book 28
The Second Book 40
The Third Book 47
The Fourth Book.. 58
The Fifth Book 76
The Sixth Book.. 93
The Seventh Book 111
The Eighth Book.. 130
The Ninth Book 149
The Tenth Book 166
The Eleventh Book 185
The Twelfth Book 200
Appendix 212
Notes.. 234
Glossary 240

Biography of Marcus Aurelius

Introduction

Throughout history, the wisdom of extraordinary individuals has reverberated, captivating the minds of generations long after their time. Marcus Aurelius stands tall among these lights, his life and beliefs echoing through ancient hallways. From 161 to 180 AD, Marcus Aurelius Antoninus, a Stoic philosopher, ruled as emperor of Rome. Historians denote that he was born in 121 AD to a prominent Roman family, presenting him an opportunity to be educated in law, philosophy, and rhetoric. He was the last emperor, known as the Five Good Emperors, and the final head of state of the Roman Empire during the Pax Romana, which lasted from 27 BC to 180 AD and was a time of comparatively calm, stability, and peace. His book, *Meditations*, leads its readers on a profound journey of self-discovery and introspection, transcending time. Widely celebrated as its author, his remarkable work boasts an enduring legacy. This foreword aims to provide a comprehensive and detailed exploration of the life and enduring legacy of Marcus Aurelius, shedding light on the man behind the masterpiece.

The Early Years

In Rome, a child named Marcus Aurelius graced the world when he was born on April 26th, 121 AD. Allegiance to a prosperous and highly-regarded family was gifted to him despite being born amid political and social unrest (Stephens, 2011). His spouse was Faustina the Younger, and he had children, namely Commodus, Lucilla, Marcus Annius Verus Caesar, and many others. The loss of his father, Marcus Annius Verus, who held the esteemed role of Praetor in the Roman Republic, had a lasting effect on Marcus Aurelius' character. Despite his youth during the tragedy, he was forced to endure the grief and solitude that accompanied it, shaping his future outlook and resilience. Domitia Lucilla, the mother of Marcus Aurelius, played a vital role in his upbringing after the sudden departure of his father. Her affection and dedication created a strong foundation for his success. Understanding his prodigious mind, she fostered his boundless curiosity, leading him to a lifepath of discovery and cognitive growth.

Apollonius of Chalcedon began to influence Marcus Aurelius as he matured due to showing intelligence that surpassed his peers from a young age. His investigation of speech, writing, and ethics demonstrated an unquenchable thirst for knowledge. Through Apollonius' mentorship and philosophical teachings, Marcus Aurelius' character was imbued with honor, fortitude, and ethical righteousness (Stephens, 2011). His worldview was deeply affected by Stoic philosophy, which instilled in him an unshakeable moral compass that guided his decisions throughout his existence. The tenets of Stoicism prioritized the development of one's values through conformity to the natural order of things. To live a fulfilling life, self-control, rationality, and acknowledgment of the inevitability of certain uncontrollable events were crucial. As Marcus Aurelius matured, his philosophical pursuits increasingly intertwined with his daily life. He endeavored to align his thoughts, actions, and intentions with the Stoic ideals he embraced, striving to embody wisdom, justice, courage, and temperance. This deep commitment to philosophical principles would define his reign as emperor and serve as a guiding light in times of adversity.

The Ascension to Power

In 138 AD, Marcus Aurelius's life took a momentous turn when his intellectual prowess and potential caught the attention of Antoninus Pius, the reigning emperor of Rome. Recognizing Marcus's exceptional abilities, Antoninus Pius adopted him as his son and designated heir, effectively securing a seamless succession of power. This unexpected twist of fate would shape the trajectory of Marcus Aurelius's life and set him on the path to becoming one of Rome's most revered emperors (Aurelius, 1905). The adoption by Antoninus Pius marked a significant honor for Marcus Aurelius, as it positioned him as the direct successor to the imperial throne. This act of adoption not only established a familial bond between the two and demonstrated Antoninus Pius's belief in Marcus's capabilities and the potential for his leadership. Under Antoninus Pius's guidance, Marcus Aurelius received an outstanding education, immersing himself in the knowledge and wisdom of the time. Upon the death of Antoninus Pius in 161 AD, Marcus Aurelius, alongside his adoptive brother

Lucius Verus, ascended to co-emperor of Rome. This joint reign presented them with a myriad of internal and external challenges. Domestically, the Roman Empire faced political unrest and social upheaval, while externally, military campaigns and territorial conflicts demanded attention and strategic prowess.

With an unwavering determination and a profound sense of duty, Marcus Aurelius embraced his duty as emperor, even facing various challenges. For him, the responsibility bestowed upon him was immense as he dedicated himself to the empire's and its people's welfare. Justice and fairness were his guiding principles as he tried to create a conducive atmosphere where everyone could live and flourish (Birley, 2000). However, the joint rule of Marcus Aurelius and Lucius Verus had its fair share of difficulties. From Britannia to the Land of the Pharaohs, the vast and vibrant empire the two royals governed left them with immense responsibility. The eastern front, especially the clashes with the Parthians, presented them with a difficult obstacle, calling for sharp tactical insights and efficient resource management. Leading by example, Marcus Aurelius demonstrated his commitment to Stoic principles and displayed remarkable fortitude and resilience throughout his reign. In his efforts to defend the empire and its citizens, Marcus Aurelius frequently joined his troops in battle and fought alongside them. This boosted morale and displayed his strong commitment to the cause. Despite the challenges of his position, he never wavered in his dedication to personal growth and enlightenment, relying on the principles of Stoicism to guide his conduct. Marcus Aurelius persisted in his philosophical pursuits while immersed in military campaigns (Birley, 2000). Marked by numerous obstacles throughout his reign, Marcus Aurelius remained steadfast in his devotion to the betterment of his subjects. His leadership was influenced by a deep commitment to intellectual and moral growth that defined his character. His policies advocated for justice and fair treatment for all, including enslaved individuals, striving for societal improvement. His compassionate and equitable approach to governance had a lasting impact on the Roman Empire, contributing to developing a more just and inclusive society.

The Philosopher-Emperor

Unlike any other emperor, Marcus Aurelius's rule was shaped by his intense passion for philosophy and Stoicism. He was a sovereign and devoted philosopher who remained committed to his principles. Despite the heavy burden of leading the Roman Empire, he led with sagacity and ethical integrity, informed by his understanding of Stoicism. These lessons governed his life and governance, bearing witness to Stoicism's guiding force over his thoughts, emotions, and behaviors. The pursuit of wisdom and the development of personal virtue was highly valued by philosopher-emperor Marcus Aurelius, who followed the pillars of Stoicism (Cavanna, 2019). For him, true happiness was not found in material possessions or authority but in the internal balance of the soul and ethical adherence. Stoicism offered him a framework to master his emotions, maintain inner tranquility, and align his actions with reason and virtue.

Marcus Aurelius's philosophy of Stoicism was a continual influence on his life. He took his role seriously as an emperor, striving to lead justly, with empathy and impartiality. Stoic beliefs underpinned his perspective, guaranteeing his judgments were reasonable, moral, and best for the empire (Cavanna, 2019). Demonstrating wisdom, bravery, temperance, and fairness, Marcus Aurelius modeled virtues for his citizens, spurring them to pursue honorable conduct and internal fortitude. But his dedication to philosophy was not purely academic. According to him, pursuing wisdom demanded a constant examination of thoughts and actions, coupled with self-reflection and discipline. As an everyday practice, he actively employed Stoic teachings as practical tools to cultivate moral excellence. By engaging in rigorous self-examination, Marcus Aurelius sought to align his character with the ideals of Stoicism, striving for self-improvement and attaining inner tranquility.

In the face of the numerous challenges confronting his reign, Marcus Aurelius turned to Stoic principles for guidance and strength. Stoicism offered him a framework to navigate adversity, teaching him to accept life's inevitable challenges with stability and resilience. Whether dealing with political conflicts, military campaigns, or personal setbacks, Marcus Aurelius maintained his composure and remained steadfast in his commitment to virtue. Stoicism gave him the tools to confront adversity calmly and rationally, enabling him to lead the empire with grace and wisdom. Beyond his personal life, Marcus Aurelius sought to disseminate the teachings of Stoicism and promote its ideals throughout the Roman Empire. He recognized the transformative potential of philosophy in shaping individuals and society. His reign witnessed the promotion of Stoic principles as a means to guide the moral conduct of his subjects and foster a sense of unity and civic responsibility. By embracing Stoicism, Marcus Aurelius aimed to cultivate a society that valued moral integrity, resilience, and the pursuit of wisdom.

Meditations

In between the turbulent responsibilities of his rule, Marcus Aurelius discovered a peaceful outlet in writing. His thoughts and musings were initially scribbled down as personal observations and eventually fused into the spectacular 'Meditations,' presenting an open window into his intellectual ponderings and inner turmoil (Aurelius, 1905). Inside each thought-provoking chapter, Marcus Aurelius expounds upon the notions of goodness, introspection, and the impermanent essence of existence. Embracing tranquility in adversity while improving oneself morally and emotionally is the essence of what 'Meditation' represents. Through reflection, the book wants us to understand our values and choices intimately, pushing us toward becoming better versions of ourselves. The book wants us to gain this more profound knowledge of the world and ourselves by introspecting.

Reflecting upon the impermanence of human existence, one of the recurring themes in "Meditations" is the transitory nature of life. Embracing the present moment is emphasized by Marcus Aurelius. He reminds readers that all things are subject to flux and that true happiness can be found by accepting and adapting to the inevitable flux of the world. In the face of adversity, Marcus Aurelius advocates cultivating inner tranquility (Aurelius, 1905). He acknowledges the challenges and hardships inherent in the human experience, urging individuals to develop resilience and inner strength. Through Stoic principles, he teaches readers to detach themselves from external circumstances and find peace and tranquility. "Meditations" also serves as a testament to the profound struggles and personal conflicts that Marcus Aurelius grappled with. In these writings, he candidly explores his imperfections and shortcomings, acknowledging his difficulties in living up to the ideals he espoused (Brummer, 2018). This vulnerability and self-awareness demonstrate his profound commitment to personal growth and the constant striving for moral excellence. The enduring appeal of "Meditations" lies in its universal wisdom and practical guidance. The writings of Marcus Aurelius provide readers with a road map for navigating life's complexity, inspiring them to cultivate virtues, face their limitations, and find comfort in the strength of reason and introspection. It pushes people to adopt a resilient and accepting worldview, empowering them to live lives with more meaning and inner peace.

Legacy and Influence

Marcus Aurelius's enduring legacy extends beyond his role as an emperor and philosopher. His moral teachings and philosophical insights resonate with readers across generations and cultures. His emphasis on personal ethics, resilience, and introspection has firmly established him as one of history's most revered thinkers and moral exemplars. Marcus Aurelius contributed to philosophy and the Roman Empire (Brummer, 2018). He committed himself to fortifying its defenses, directing fruitful military campaigns, and establishing laws and social reforms to enhance the lives of his subjects. His dedication to fairness, compassion, and treating all people equally, even enslaved people, aided in developing a more just society.

Conclusion

As readers embark on the journey through the profound insights of Marcus Aurelius in 'Meditations,' they have the privilege of accompanying an extraordinary individual who embodies the ideals of wisdom, virtue, and introspection. Marcus Aurelius's remarkable life and enduring legacy testify to the boundless potential for personal growth and moral enlightenment within each of us. May his words inspire us to cultivate inner tranquility, embrace virtue, and strive for a life well-lived. May his words continue to be adopted by many people so that people can live a life that the incoming generations can admire.

References

Aurelius, M. (1905). *The meditations of the emperor Marcus Aurelius Antoninus*. Methuen.

Brummer, S. (2018). *Marcus Aurelius: Living philosophy and the business of governing an Empire* (Doctoral dissertation, Stellenbosch: Stellenbosch University).

Birley, A. (2000). *Marcus Aurelius: a biography*. Psychology Press.

Cavanna, A. E. (2019). Stoic philosophy and psychotherapy: Implications for neuropsychiatric conditions. *Dialogues in Philosophy, Mental & Neuro Sciences, 12(1)*.

Stephens, W. O. (2011). *Marcus Aurelius: A guide for the perplexed*. A&C Black.

INTRODUCTION

MARCUS AURELIUS ANTONINUS was born on April 26, A.D. 121. His real name was M. Annius Verus, and he was sprung of a noble family which claimed descent from Numa, second King of Rome. Thus the most religious of emperors came of the blood of the most pious of early kings. His father, Annius Verus, had held high office in Rome, and his grandfather, of the same name, had been thrice Consul. Both his parents died young, but Marcus held them in loving remembrance. On his father's death Marcus was adopted by his grandfather, the consular Annius Verus, and there was deep love between these two. On the very first page of his book Marcus gratefully declares how of his grandfather he had learned to be gentle and meek, and to refrain from all anger and passion. The Emperor Hadrian divined the fine character of the lad, whom he used to call not Verus but Verissimus, more Truthful than his own name. He advanced Marcus to equestrian rank when six years of age, and at the age of eight made him a member of the ancient Salian priesthood. The boy's aunt, Annia Galeria Faustina, was married to Antoninus Pius, afterwards emperor. Hence it came about that Antoninus, having no son, adopted Marcus, changing his name to that which he is known by, and betrothed him to his daughter Faustina. His education was conducted with all care. The ablest teachers were engaged for him, and he was trained in the strict doctrine of the Stoic philosophy, which was his great delight. He was taught to dress plainly and to live simply, to avoid all softness and luxury. His body was trained to hardihood by wrestling, hunting, and outdoor games; and though his constitution was weak, he showed great personal courage to encounter the fiercest boars. At the same time he was kept from the extravagancies of his day. The great excitement in Rome was the strife of the Factions, as they were called, in the circus. The racing drivers used to adopt one of four colours—red, blue, white, or green—and their partisans showed an eagerness in supporting them which nothing could surpass. Riot and corruption went in the train of the racing chariots; and from all these things Marcus held severely aloof.

In 140 Marcus was raised to the consulship, and in 145 his betrothal was consummated by marriage. Two years later Faustina brought him a daughter; and soon after the tribunate and other imperial honours were conferred upon him.

Antoninus Pius died in 161, and Marcus assumed the imperial state. He at once associated with himself L. Ceionius Commodus, whom Antoninus had adopted as a younger son at the same time with Marcus, giving him the name of Lucius Aurelius Verus. Henceforth the two are colleagues in the empire, the junior being trained as it were to succeed. No sooner was Marcus settled upon the throne than wars broke out on all sides. In the east, Vologeses III. of Parthia began a long-meditated revolt by destroying a whole Roman Legion and invading Syria (162). Verus was sent off in hot haste to quell this rising; and he fulfilled his trust by plunging into drunkenness and debauchery, while the war was left to his officers. Soon after Marcus had to face a more serious danger at home in the coalition of several powerful tribes on the northern frontier. Chief among those were the Marcomanni or Marchmen, the Quadi (mentioned in this book), the Sarmatians, the Catti, the Jazyges. In Rome itself there was pestilence and starvation, the one brought from the east by Verus's legions, the other caused by floods which had destroyed vast quantities of grain. After all had been done possible to allay famine and to supply pressing needs—Marcus being forced even to sell the imperial jewels to find money—both emperors set forth to a struggle which was to continue more or less during the rest of Marcus's reign. During these wars, in 169, Verus died. We have no means of following the campaigns in detail; but thus much is certain, that in the end the Romans succeeded in crushing the barbarian tribes, and effecting a settlement which made the empire more secure. Marcus was himself commander-in-chief, and victory was due no less to his own ability than to his wisdom in choice of lieutenants, shown conspicuously in the case of Pertinax. There were several important battles fought in these campaigns; and one of them has become celebrated for the legend of the Thundering Legion. In a battle against the Quadi in 174, the day seemed to be going in favour of the foe, when on a sudden arose a great storm of thunder and rain the lightning struck the barbarians with terror, and they turned to rout. In later days this storm was said to have been sent in answer to the prayers of a legion which contained many Christians, and the name Thundering Legion should be given to it on this account. The title of Thundering Legion is known at an earlier date, so this part of the story at least cannot be true; but the aid of the storm is acknowledged by one of the scenes carved on Antonine's Column at Rome, which commemorates these wars.

Meditations

The settlement made after these troubles might have been more satisfactory but for an unexpected rising in the east. Avidius Cassius, an able captain who had won renown in the Parthian wars, was at this time chief governor of the eastern provinces. By whatever means induced, he had conceived the project of proclaiming himself emperor as soon as Marcus, who was then in feeble health, should die; and a report having been conveyed to him that Marcus was dead, Cassius did as he had planned. Marcus, on hearing the news, immediately patched up a peace and returned home to meet this new peril. The emperors great grief was that he must needs engage in the horrors of civil strife. He praised the qualities of Cassius, and expressed a heartfelt wish that Cassius might not be driven to do himself a hurt before he should have the opportunity to grant a free pardon. But before he could come to the east news had come to Cassius that the emperor still lived; his followers fell away from him, and he was assassinated. Marcus now went to the east, and while there the murderers brought the head of Cassius to him; but the emperor indignantly refused their gift, nor would he admit the men to his presence.

On this journey his wife, Faustina, died. At his return the emperor celebrated a triumph (176). Immediately afterwards he repaired to Germany, and took up once more the burden of war. His operations were followed by complete success; but the troubles of late years had been too much for his constitution, at no time robust, and on March 17, 180, he died in Pannonia.

The good emperor was not spared domestic troubles. Faustina had borne him several children, of whom he was passionately fond. Their innocent faces may still be seen in many a sculpture gallery, recalling with odd effect the dreamy countenance of their father. But they died one by one, and when Marcus came to his own end only one of his sons still lived—the weak and worthless Commodus. On his father's death Commodus, who succeeded him, undid the work of many campaigns by a hasty and unwise peace; and his reign of twelve years proved him to be a ferocious and bloodthirsty tyrant. Scandal has made free with the name of Faustina herself, who is accused not only of unfaithfulness, but of intriguing with Cassius and egging him on to his fatal rebellion, it must be admitted that these charges rest on no sure evidence; and the emperor, at all events, loved her dearly, nor ever felt the slightest qualm of suspicion.

As a soldier we have seen that Marcus was both capable and successful; as an administrator he was prudent and conscientious. Although steeped in the teachings of philosophy, he did not attempt to remodel the world on any preconceived plan. He trod the path beaten by his predecessors, seeking only to do his duty as well as he could, and to keep out corruption. He did some unwise things, it is true. To create a compeer in empire, as he did with Verus, was a dangerous innovation which could only succeed if one of the two effaced himself; and under Diocletian this very precedent caused the Roman Empire to split into halves. He erred in his civil administration by too much centralising. But the strong point of his reign was the administration of justice. Marcus sought by-laws to protect the weak, to make the lot of the slaves less hard, to stand in place of father to the fatherless. Charitable foundations were endowed for rearing and educating poor children. The provinces were protected against oppression, and public help was given to cities or districts which might be visited by calamity.

The great blot on his name, and one hard indeed to explain, is his treatment of the Christians. In his reign Justin at Rome became a martyr to his faith, and Polycarp at Smyrna, and we know of many outbreaks of fanaticism in the provinces which caused the death of the faithful. It is no excuse to plead that he knew nothing about the atrocities done in his name: it was his duty to know, and if he did not he would have been the first to confess that he had failed in his duty. But from his own tone in speaking of the Christians it is clear he knew them only from calumny; and we hear of no measures taken even to secure that they should have a fair hearing. In this respect Trajan was better than he.

To a thoughtful mind such a religion as that of Rome would give small satisfaction. Its legends were often childish or impossible; its teaching had little to do with morality. The Roman religion was in fact of the nature of a bargain: men paid certain sacrifices and rites, and the gods granted their favour, irrespective of right or wrong. In this case all devout souls were thrown back upon philosophy, as they had been, though to a less extent, in Greece. There were under the early empire two rival schools which practically divided the field between them, Stoicism and Epicureanism. The ideal set before each was nominally much the same. The Stoics aspired to ἀπάθεια, the repression of all emotion, and the Epicureans to ἀταραξία, freedom from all disturbance; yet in the upshot the one has become a synonym of stubborn endurance, the other for unbridled licence. With Epicureanism we have nothing to do now; but it will be worth while to sketch the history and tenets of the Stoic sect.

Zeno, the founder of Stoicism, was born in Cyprus at some date unknown, but his life may be said roughly to be between the years 350 and 250 B.C. Cyprus has been from time immemorial a meeting-place of the East and West, and although we cannot grant any importance to a possible strain of Phœnician blood in him (for the Phoenicians were no philosophers), yet it is quite likely that through Asia Minor he may have come in touch with the Far East. He studied under the cynic Crates, but he did not neglect other philosophical systems. After many years' study he opened his own school in a colonnade in Athens called the Painted Porch, or Stoa, which gave the Stoics their name. Next to Zeno, the School of the Porch owes most to Chrysippus (280—207 b.c.), who organised Stoicism into a system. Of him it was said,

'But for Chrysippus, there had been no Porch.'

The Stoics regarded speculation as a means to an end and that end was, as Zeno put it, to live consistently (ὁμολογουμένος ζῆν), or as it was later explained, to live in conformity with nature (ὁμολογουμένος τῇ φύσει ζῆν). This conforming of the life to nature was the Stoic idea of Virtue. This dictum might easily be taken to mean that virtue consists in yielding to each natural impulse; but that was very far from the Stoic meaning. In order to live in accord with nature, it is necessary to know what nature is; and to this end a threefold division of philosophy is made—into *Physics*, dealing with the universe and its laws, the problems of divine government and teleology; *Logic*, which trains the mind to discern true from false; and *Ethics*, which applies the knowledge thus gained and tested to practical life.

The Stoic system of physics was materialism with an infusion of pantheism. In contradiction to Plato's view that the Ideas, or Prototypes, of phenomena alone really

16

exist, the Stoics held that material objects alone existed; but immanent in the material universe was a spiritual force which acted through them, manifesting itself under many forms, as fire, æther, spirit, soul, reason, the ruling principle.

The universe, then, is God, of whom the popular gods are manifestations; while legends and myths are allegorical. The soul of man is thus an emanation from the godhead, into whom it will eventually be re-absorbed. The divine ruling principle makes all things work together for good, but for the good of the whole. The highest good of man is consciously to work with God for the common good, and this is the sense in which the Stoic tried to live in accord with nature. In the individual it is virtue alone which enables him to do this; as Providence rules the universe, so virtue in the soul must rule man.

In Logic, the Stoic system is noteworthy for their theory as to the test of truth, the *Criterion*. They compared the new-born soul to a sheet of paper ready for writing. Upon this the senses write their impressions (φαντασίαι), and by experience of a number of these the soul unconsciously conceives general notions (κοιναὶ ἔννοιαι) or anticipations (προλήψεις). When the impression was such as to be irresistible it was called (καταληπτικὴ φαντασία) one that holds fast, or as they explained it, one proceeding from truth. Ideas and inferences artificially produced by deduction or the like were tested by this 'holding perception.' Of the Ethical application I have already spoken. The highest good was the virtuous life. Virtue alone is happiness, and vice is unhappiness. Carrying this theory to its extreme, the Stoic said that there could be no gradations between virtue and vice, though of course each has its special manifestations.

Moreover, nothing is good but virtue, and nothing but vice is bad. Those outside things which are commonly called good or bad, such as health and sickness, wealth and poverty, pleasure and pain, are to him indifferent (ἀδιάφορα). All these things are merely the sphere in which virtue may act. The ideal Wise Man is sufficient unto himself in all things (αὐταρκής); and knowing these truths, he will be happy even when stretched upon the rack. It is probable that no Stoic claimed for himself that he was this Wise Man, but that each strove after it as an ideal much as the Christian strives after a likeness to Christ. The exaggeration in this statement was, however, so obvious, that the later Stoics were driven to make a further subdivision of things indifferent into what is preferable (προηγμένα) and what is undesirable (ἀποπροηγμένα). They also held that for him who had not attained to the perfect wisdom, certain actions were proper. (καθήκοντα) These were neither virtuous nor vicious, but, like the indifferent things, held a middle place.

Two points in the Stoic system deserve special mention. One is a careful distinction between things which are in our power and things which are not. Desire and dislike, opinion and affection, are within the power of the will; whereas health, wealth, honour, and other such are generally not so. The Stoic was called upon to control his desires and affections, and to guide his opinion; to bring his whole being under the sway of the will or leading principle, just as the universe is guided and governed by divine Providence. This is a special application of the favourite Greek virtue of moderation (σωφροσύνη), and has also its parallel in Christian ethics. The second point is a strong insistence on the unity of the universe, and on man's duty as part of a great whole.

Public spirit was the most splendid political virtue of the ancient world, and it is here made cosmopolitan. It is again instructive to note that Christian sages insisted on the same thing. Christians are taught that they are members of a worldwide brotherhood, where is neither Greek nor Hebrew, bond nor free and that they live their lives as fellow-workers with God.

Such is the system which underlies the Meditations of Marcus Aurelius. Some knowledge of it is necessary to the right understanding of the book, but for us the chief interest lies elsewhere. We do not come to Marcus Aurelius for a treatise on Stoicism. He is no head of a school to lay down a body of doctrine for students; he does not even contemplate that others should read what he writes. His philosophy is not an eager intellectual inquiry, but more what we should call religious feeling. The uncompromising stiffness of Zeno or Chrysippus is softened and transformed by passing through a nature reverent and tolerant, gentle and free from guile; the grim resignation which made life possible to the Stoic sage becomes in him almost a mood of aspiration. His book records the innermost thoughts of his heart, set down to ease it, with such moral maxims and reflections as may help him to bear the burden of duty and the countless annoyances of a busy life.

It is instructive to compare the *Meditations* with another famous book, the *Imitation of Christ*. There is the same ideal of self-control in both. It should be a man's task, says the *Imitation*, 'to overcome himself, and every day to be stronger than himself.' 'In withstanding of the passions standeth very peace of heart.' 'Let us set the axe to the root, that we being purged of our passions may have a peaceable mind.' To this end there must be continual self-examination. 'If thou may not continually gather thyself together, namely sometimes do it, at least once a day, the morning or the evening. In the morning purpose, in the evening discuss the manner, what thou hast been this day, in word, work, and thought.' But while the Roman's temper is a modest self-reliance, the Christian aims at a more passive mood, humbleness and meekness, and reliance on the presence and personal friendship of God. The Roman scrutinises his faults with severity, but without the self-contempt which makes the Christian 'vile in his own sight.' The Christian, like the Roman, bids 'study to withdraw thine heart from the love of things visible'; but it is not the busy life of duty he has in mind so much as the contempt of all worldly things, and the 'cutting away of all lower delectations.' Both rate men's praise or blame at their real worthlessness; 'Let not thy peace,' says the Christian, 'be in the mouths of men.' But it is to God's censure the Christian appeals, the Roman to his own soul. The petty annoyances of injustice or unkindness are looked on by each with the same magnanimity. 'Why doth a little thing said or done against thee make thee sorry? It is no new thing; it is not the first, nor shall it be the last, if thou live long. At best suffer patiently, if thou canst not suffer joyously.' The Christian should sorrow more for other men's malice than for our own wrongs; but the Roman is inclined to wash his hands of the offender. 'Study to be patient in suffering and bearing other men's defaults and all manner infirmities,' says the Christian; but the Roman would never have thought to add, 'If all men were perfect, what had we then to suffer of other men for God?' The virtue of suffering in itself is an idea which does not meet us in the *Meditations*. Both alike realise that man is one of a great community. 'No man is sufficient to himself,' says the Christian; 'we must bear together, help together, comfort together.' But while he sees a chief importance in zeal, in exalted emotion that is, and avoidance of lukewarmness, the Roman thought mainly of the duty to be done as well as might be, and less of the feeling which should go with the doing of it. To the saint as to the emperor, the world is a poor thing at best. 'Verily it is a misery to live upon the earth,' says the Christian; few and evil are the days of man's life, which passeth away suddenly as a shadow.

But there is one great difference between the two books we are considering. The *Imitation* is addressed to others, the *Meditations* by the writer to himself. We learn nothing from the *Imitation* of the author's own life, except in so far as he may be assumed to have practised his own preachings; the *Meditations* reflect mood by mood the mind of him who wrote them. In their intimacy and frankness lies their great charm. These notes are not sermons; they are not even confessions. There is always an air of self-consciousness in confessions; in such revelations there is always a danger of unctuousness or of vulgarity for the best of men. St. Augus-tine is not always clear of offence, and John Bunyan himself exaggerates venial peccadilloes into heinous sins. But Marcus Aurelius is neither vulgar nor unctuous; he extenuates nothing, but nothing sets down in malice. He never poses before an audience; he may not be profound, he is always sincere. And it is a lofty and serene soul which is here disclosed before us. Vulgar vices seem to have no temptation for him; this is not one tied and bound with chains which he strives to break. The faults he detects in himself are often such as most men would have no eyes to see. To serve the divine spirit which is implanted within him, a man must 'keep himself pure from all violent passion and evil affection, from all rashness and vanity, and from all manner of discontent, either in regard of the gods or men': or, as he says elsewhere, 'unspotted by pleasure, undaunted by pain.' Unwavering courtesy and consideration are his aims. 'Whatsoever any man either doth or saith, thou must be good;' 'doth any man offend? It is against himself that he doth offend: why should it trouble thee?' The offender needs pity, not wrath; those who must needs be corrected, should be treated with tact and gentleness; and one must be always ready to learn better. 'The best kind of revenge is, not to become like unto them.' There are so many hints of offence forgiven, that we may believe the notes followed sharp on the facts. Perhaps he has fallen short of his aim, and thus seeks to call his principles to mind, and to strengthen himself for the future. That these sayings are not mere talk is plain from the story of Avidius Cassius, who would have usurped his imperial throne. Thus the emperor faithfully carries out his own principle, that evil must be overcome with good. For each fault in others, Nature (says he) has given us a counteracting virtue; 'as, for example, against the unthankful, it hath given goodness and meekness, as an antidote.'

One so gentle towards a foe was sure to be a good friend; and indeed his pages are full of generous gratitude to those who had served him. In his First Book he sets down to account all the debts due to his kinsfolk and teachers. To his grandfather he owed his own gentle spirit, to his father shamefastness and courage; he learnt of his mother to be religious and bountiful and single-minded. Rusticus did not work in vain, if he showed his pupil that his life needed amending. Apollonius taught him simplicity, reasonableness, gratitude, a love of true liberty. So the list runs on; every one he had dealings with seems to have given him something good, a sure proof of the goodness of his nature, which thought no evil.

If his was that honest and true heart which is the Christian ideal, this is the more wonderful in that he lacked the faith which makes Christians strong. He could say, it is true, 'either there is a God, and then all is well; or if all things go by chance and fortune, yet mayest thou use thine own providence in those things that concern thee properly; and then art thou well.' Or again, 'We must needs grant that there is a nature that doth govern the universe.' But his own part in the scheme of things is so small, that he does not hope for any personal happiness beyond what a serene soul may win in this mortal life. 'O my soul, the time I trust will be, when thou shalt be good, simple, more open and visible, than that body by which it is enclosed;' but this is said of the calm contentment with human lot which he hopes to attain, not of a time when the trammels of the body shall be cast off. For the rest, the world and its fame and wealth, 'all is vanity.' The gods may perhaps have a particular care for him, but their especial care is for the universe at large: thus much should suffice. His gods are better than the Stoic gods, who sit aloof from all human things, untroubled and uncaring, but his personal hope is hardly stronger. On this point he says little, though there are many allusions to death as the natural end; doubtless he expected his soul one day to be absorbed into the universal soul, since nothing comes out of nothing, and nothing can be annihilated. His mood is one of strenuous weariness; he does his duty as a good soldier, waiting for the sound of the trumpet which shall sound the retreat; he has not that cheerful confidence which led Socrates through a life no less noble, to a death which was to bring him into the company of gods he had worshipped and men whom he had revered.

But although Marcus Aurelius may have held intellectually that his soul was destined to be absorbed, and to lose consciousness of itself, there were times when he felt, as all who hold it must sometimes feel, how unsatisfying is such a creed. Then he gropes blindly after something less empty and vain. 'Thou hast taken ship,' he says, 'thou hast sailed, thou art come to land, go out, if to another life, there also shalt thou find gods, who are everywhere.' There is more in this than the assumption of a rival theory for argument's sake. If worldly things 'be but as a dream, the thought is not far off that there may be an awakening to what is real. When he speaks of death as a necessary change, and points out that nothing useful and profitable can be brought about without change, did he perhaps think of the change in a corn of wheat, which is not quickened except it die? Nature's marvellous power of recreating out of Corruption is surely not confined to bodily things. Many of his thoughts sound like far-off echoes of St. Paul; and it is strange indeed that this most Christian of emperors has nothing good to say of the Christians. To him they are only sectaries 'violently and passionately set upon opposition.

Profound as philosophy these *Meditations* certainly are not; but Marcus Aurelius was too sincere not to see the essence of such things as came within his experience. Ancient religions were for the most part concerned with outward things. Do the necessary rites, and you propitiate the gods; and these rites were often trivial, sometimes violated right feeling or even morality. Even when the gods stood on the side of righteousness, they were concerned with the act more than with the intent. But Marcus Aurelius knows that what the heart is full of, the man will do. 'Such as thy thoughts and ordinary cogitations are,' he says, 'such will thy mind be in time.'

And every page of the book shows us that he knew thought was sure to issue in act. He drills his soul, as it were, in right principles, that when the time comes, it may be guided by them. To wait until the emergency is to be too late.

He sees also the true essence of happiness. 'If happiness did consist in pleasure, how came notorious robbers, impure abominable livers, parricides, and tyrants, in so large a measure to have their part of pleasures?' He who had all the world's pleasures at command can write thus 'A happy lot and portion is, good inclinations of the soul, good desires, good actions.'

By the irony of fate this man, so gentle and good, so desirous of quiet joys and a mind free from care, was set at the head of the Roman Empire when great dangers threatened from east and west. For several years he himself commanded his armies in chief. In camp before the Quadi he dates the first book of his *Meditations*, and shows how he could retire within himself amid the coarse clangour of arms. The pomps and glories which he despised were all his; what to most men is an ambition or a dream, to him was a round of weary tasks which nothing but the stern sense of duty could carry him through. And he did his work well. His wars were slow and tedious, but successful. With a statesman's wisdom he foresaw the danger to Rome of the barbarian hordes from the north, and took measures to meet it. As it was, his settlement gave two centuries of respite to the Roman Empire; had he fulfilled the plan of pushing the imperial frontiers to the Elbe, which seems to have been in his mind, much more might have been accomplished. But death cut short his designs.

Truly a rare opportunity was given to Marcus Aurelius of showing what the mind can do in despite of circumstances. Most peaceful of warriors, a magnificent monarch whose ideal was quiet happiness in home life, bent to obscurity yet born to greatness, the loving father of children who died young or turned out hateful, his life was one paradox. That nothing might lack, it was in camp before the face of the enemy that he passed away and went to his own place.

The following is a list of the chief English translations of Marcus Aurelius: (1) By Meric Casaubon, 1634; (2) Jeremy Collier, 1701; (3) James Thomson, 1747; (4) R. Graves, 1792; (5) H. McCormac, 1844; (6) George Long, 1862; (7) G. H. Rendall, 1898; and (8) J. Jackson, 1906. Renan's "Marc-Aurèle"—in his "History of the Origins of Christianity," which appeared in 1882—is the most vital and original book to be had relating to the time of Marcus Aurelius. Pater's "Marius the Epicurean" forms another outside commentary, which is of service in the imaginative attempt to create again the period.

HIS FIRST BOOK

Concerning HIMSELF:

Wherein Antoninus recordeth, What and of whom, whether Parents, Friends, or Masters; by their good examples, or good advice and counsel, he had learned:

Divided into Numbers or Sections.

ANTONINUS Book vi. Num. xlviii. Whensoever thou wilt rejoice thyself, think and meditate upon those good parts and especial gifts, which thou hast observed in any of them that live with thee: as industry in one, in another modesty, in another bountifulness, in another some other thing. For nothing can so much rejoice thee, as the resemblances and parallels of several virtues, eminent in the dispositions of them that live with thee, especially when all at once, as it were, they represent themselves unto thee. See therefore, that thou have them always in a readiness.

THE FIRST BOOK

I. Of my grandfather Verus I have learned to be gentle and meek, and to refrain from all anger and passion. From the fame and memory of him that begot me I have learned both shamefastness and manlike behaviour. Of my mother I have learned to be religious, and bountiful; and to forbear, not only to do, but to intend any evil; to content myself with a spare diet, and to fly all such excess as is incidental to great wealth. Of my great-grandfather, both to frequent public schools and auditories, and to get me good and able teachers at home; and that I ought not to think much, if upon such occasions, I were at excessive charges.

II. Of him that brought me up, not to be fondly addicted to either of the two great factions of the coursers in the circus, called Prasini, and Veneti: nor in the amphitheatre partially to favour any of the gladiators, or fencers, as either the Parmularii, or the Secutores. Moreover, to endure labour; nor to need many things; when I have anything to do, to do it myself rather than by others; not to meddle with many businesses; and not easily to admit of any slander.

III. Of Diognetus, not to busy myself about vain things, and not easily to believe those things, which are commonly spoken, by such as take upon them to work wonders, and by sorcerers, or prestidigitators, and impostors; concerning the power of charms, and their driving out of demons, or evil spirits; and the like. Not to keep quails for the game; nor to be mad after such things. Not to be offended with other men's liberty of speech, and to apply myself unto philosophy. Him also I must thank, that ever I heard first Bacchius, then Tandasis and Marcianus, and that I did write dialogues in my youth; and that I took liking to the philosophers' little couch and skins, and such other things, which by the Grecian discipline are proper to those who profess philosophy.

IV. To Rusticus I am beholding, that I first entered into the conceit that my life wanted some redress and cure. And then, that I did not fall into the ambition of ordinary sophists, either to write tracts concerning the common theorems, or to exhort men unto virtue and the study of philosophy by public orations; as also that I never by way of ostentation did affect to show myself an active able man, for any kind of bodily exercises. And that I gave over the study of rhetoric and poetry, and of elegant neat language. That I did not use to walk about the house in my long robe, nor to do any such things. Moreover I learned of him to write letters without any affectation, or curiosity; such as that was, which by him was written to my mother from Sinuessa: and to be easy and ready to be reconciled, and well pleased again with them that had offended me, as soon as any of them would be content to seek unto me again. To read with diligence; not to rest satisfied with a light and superficial knowledge, nor quickly to assent to things commonly spoken of: whom also I must thank that ever I lighted upon Epictetus his *Hypomnemata*, or moral commentaries and common-factions: which also he gave me of his own.

V. From Apollonius, true liberty, and unvariable steadfastness, and not to regard anything at all, though never so little, but right and reason: and always, whether in the sharpest pains, or after the loss of a child, or in long diseases, to be still the same man; who also was a present and visible example unto me, that it was possible for the same man to be both vehement and remiss: a man not subject to be vexed, and offended with the incapacity of his scholars and auditors in his lectures and expositions; and a true pattern of a man who of all his good gifts and faculties, least esteemed in himself, that his excellent skill and ability to teach and persuade others the common theorems and maxims of the Stoic philosophy. Of him also I learned how to receive favours and kindnesses (as commonly they are accounted:) from friends, so that I might not become obnoxious unto them, for them, nor more yielding upon occasion, than in right I ought; and yet so that I should not pass them neither, as an unsensible and unthankful man.

VI. Of Sextus, mildness and the pattern of a family governed with paternal affection; and a purpose to live according to nature: to be grave without affectation: to observe carefully the several dispositions of my friends, not to be offended with idiots, nor unseasonably to set upon those that are carried with the vulgar opinions, with the theorems, and tenets of philosophers: his conversation being an example how a man might accommodate himself to all men and companies; so that though his company were sweeter and more pleasing than any flatterer's cogging and fawning; yet was it at the same time most respected and reverenced: who also had a proper happiness and faculty, rationally and methodically to find out, and set in order all necessary determinations and instructions for a man's life. A man without ever the least appearance of anger, or any other passion; able at the same time most exactly to observe the Stoic *Apathia*, or unpassionateness, and yet to be most tender-hearted: ever of good credit; and yet almost without any noise, or rumour: very learned, and yet making little show.

VII. From Alexander the Grammarian, to be unreprovable myself, and not reproachfully to reprehend any man for a barbarism, or a solecism, or any false pronunciation, but dextrously by way of answer, or testimony, or confirmation of the same matter (taking no notice of the word) to utter it as it should have been spoken; or by some other such close and indirect admonition, handsomely and civilly to tell him of it.

VIII. Of Fronto, to how much envy and fraud and hypocrisy the state of a tyrannous king is subject unto, and how they who are commonly called εὐπατρίδαι, *i.e.* nobly born, are in some sort incapable, or void of natural affection.

IX. Of Alexander the Platonic, not often nor without great necessity to say, or to write to any man in a letter, 'I am not at leisure'; nor in this manner still to put off those duties, which we owe to our friends and acquaintances (to every one in his kind) under pretence of urgent affairs.

X. Of Catulus, not to contemn any friend's expostulation, though unjust, but to strive to reduce him to his former disposition: freely and heartily to speak well of all my masters upon any occasion, as it is reported of Domitius, and Athenodotus: and to love my children with true affection.

XI. From my brother Severus, to be kind and loving to all them of my house and family; by whom also I came to the knowledge of Thrasea and Helvidius, and Cato, and Dio, and Brutus. He it was also that did put me in the first conceit and desire of an equal commonwealth, administered by justice and equality; and of a kingdom wherein should be regarded nothing more than the good and welfare of the subjects. Of him also, to observe a constant tenor, (not interrupted, with any other cares and distractions,) in the study and esteem of philosophy: to be bountiful and liberal in the largest measure; always to hope the best; and to be confident that my friends love me. In whom I moreover observed open dealing towards those whom he reproved at any time, and that his friends might without all doubt or much observation know what he would, or would not, so open and plain was he.

XII. From Claudius Maximus, in all things to endeavour to have power of myself, and in nothing to be carried about; to be cheerful and courageous in all sudden chances and accidents, as in sicknesses: to love mildness, and moderation, and gravity: and to do my business, whatsoever it be, thoroughly, and without querulousness. Whatsoever he said, all men believed him that as he spake, so he thought, and whatsoever he did, that he did it with a good intent. His manner was, never to wonder at anything; never to be in haste, and yet never slow: nor to be perplexed, or dejected, or at any time unseemly, or excessively to laugh: nor to be angry, or suspicious, but ever ready to do good, and to forgive, and to speak truth; and all this, as one that seemed rather of himself to have been straight and right, than ever to have been rectified or redressed; neither was there any man that ever thought himself undervalued by him, or that could find in his heart, to think himself a better man than he. He would also be very pleasant and gracious.

XIII. In my father, I observed his meekness; his constancy without wavering in those things, which after a due examination and deliberation, he had determined. How free from all vanity he carried himself in matter of honour and dignity, (as they are esteemed:) his laboriousness and assiduity, his readiness to hear any man, that had aught to say tending to any common good: how generally and impartially he would give every man his due; his skill and knowledge, when rigour or extremity, or when remissness or moderation was in season; how he did abstain from all unchaste love of youths; his moderate condescending to other men's occasions as an ordinary man, neither absolutely requiring of his friends, that they should wait upon him at his ordinary meals, nor that they should of necessity accompany him in his journeys; and that whensoever any business upon some necessary occasions was to be put off and omitted before it could be ended, he was ever found when he went about it again, the same man that he was before. His accurate examination of things in consultations, and patient hearing of others. He would not hastily give over the search of the matter, as one easy to be satisfied with sudden notions and apprehensions. His care to preserve his friends; how neither at any time he would carry himself towards them with disdainful neglect, and grow weary of them; nor yet at any time be madly fond of them. His contented mind in all things, his cheerful countenance, his care to foresee things afar off, and to take order for the least, without any noise or clamour. Moreover how all acclamations and flattery were repressed by him: how carefully he observed all things necessary to the government, and kept an account of the common expenses, and how patiently he did abide that he was reprehended by some for this his strict and rigid kind of dealing. How he was neither a superstitious worshipper of the gods, nor an ambitious pleaser of men, or studious of popular applause; but sober in all things, and everywhere observant of that which was fitting; no affecter of novelties: in those things which conduced to his ease and convenience, (plenty whereof his fortune did afford him,) without pride and bragging, yet with all freedom and liberty: so that as he did freely enjoy them without any anxiety or affectation when they were present; so when absent, he found no want of them. Moreover, that he was never commended by any man, as either a learned acute man, or an obsequious officious man, or a fine orator; but as a ripe mature man, a perfect sound man; one that could not endure to be flattered; able to govern both himself and others. Moreover, how much he did honour all true philosophers, without upbraiding those that were not so; his sociableness, his gracious and delightful conversation, but never unto satiety; his care of his body within bounds and measure, not as one that desired to live long, or over-studious of neatness, and elegancy; and yet not as one that did not regard it: so that through his own care and providence, he seldom needed any inward physic, or outward applications: but especially how ingeniously he would yield to any that had obtained any peculiar faculty, as either eloquence, or the knowledge of the laws, or of ancient customs, or the like; and how he concurred with them, in his best care and endeavour that every one of them might in his kind, for that wherein he excelled, be regarded and esteemed: and although he did all things carefully after the ancient customs of his forefathers, yet even of this was he not desirous that men should take notice, that he did imitate ancient customs. Again, how he was not easily moved and tossed up and down, but loved to be constant, both in the same places and businesses; and how after his great fits of headache he would return fresh and vigorous to his wonted affairs. Again, that secrets he neither had many, nor often, and such only as concerned public matters: his discretion and moderation, in exhibiting of the public sights and shows for the pleasure and pastime of the people: in public buildings. congiaries, and the like. In all these things, having a respect unto men only as men, and to the equity of the things themselves, and not unto the glory that might follow. Never wont to use the baths at unseasonable hours; no builder; never curious, or solicitous, either about his meat, or about the workmanship, or colour of his clothes, or about anything that belonged to external beauty. In all his conversation, far from all inhumanity, all boldness, and incivility, all greediness and impetuosity; never doing anything with such earnestness, and intention, that a man could say of him, that he did sweat about it: but contrariwise, all things distinctly, as at leisure; without trouble; orderly, soundly, and agreeably. A man might have applied that to him, which is recorded of Socrates, that he knew how to want, and to enjoy those things, in the want whereof, most men show themselves weak; and in the fruition, intemperate: but to hold out firm and constant, and to keep within the compass of true moderation and sobriety in either estate, is proper to a man, who hath a perfect and invincible soul; such as he showed himself in the sickness of Maximus.

XIV. From the gods I received that I had good grandfathers, and parents, a good sister, good masters, good domestics, loving kinsmen, almost all that I have; and that I never through haste and rashness transgressed against any of them, notwithstanding that my disposition was such, as that such a thing (if occasion had been) might very well have been committed by me, but that It was the mercy of the gods, to prevent such a concurring of matters and occasions, as might make me to incur this blame. That I was not long brought up by the concubine of my father; that I preserved the flower of my youth. That I took not upon me to be a man before my time, but rather put it off longer than I needed. That I lived under the government of my lord and father, who would take away from me all pride and vainglory, and reduce me to that conceit and opinion that it was not impossible for a prince to live in the court without a troop of guards and followers, extraordinary apparel, such and such torches and statues, and other like particulars of state and magnificence; but that a man may reduce and contract himself almost to the state of a private man, and yet for all that not to become the more base and remiss in those public matters and affairs, wherein power and authority is requisite. That I have had such a brother, who by his own example might stir me up to think of myself; and by his respect and love, delight and please me. That I have got ingenuous children, and that they were not born distorted, nor with any other natural deformity. That I was no great proficient in the study of rhetoric and poetry, and of other faculties, which perchance I might have dwelt upon, if I had found myself to go on in them with success. That I did by times prefer those, by whom I was brought up, to such places and dignities, which they seemed unto me most to desire; and that I did not put them off with hope and expectation, that (since that they were yet but young) I would do the same hereafter. That I ever knew Apollonius and Rusticus, and Maximus. That I have had occasion often and effectually to consider and meditate with myself, concerning that life which is according to nature, what the nature and manner of it is: so that as for the gods and such suggestions, helps and inspirations, as might be expected from them, nothing did hinder, but that I might have begun long before to live according to nature; or that even now that I was not yet partaker and in present possession of that life, that I myself (in that I did not observe those inward motions, and suggestions, yea and almost plain and apparent instructions and admonitions of the gods,) was the only cause of it. That my body in such a life, hath been able to hold out so long. That I never had to do with Benedicta and Theodotus, yea and afterwards when I fell into some fits of love, I was soon cured. That having been often displeased with Rusticus, I never did him anything for which afterwards I had occasion to repent. That it being so that my mother was to die young, yet she lived with me all her latter years. That as often as I had a purpose to help and succour any that either were poor, or fallen into some present necessity, I never was answered by my officers that there was not ready money enough to do it; and that I myself never had occasion to require the like succour from any other. That I have such a wife, so obedient, so loving, so ingenuous. That I had choice of fit and able men, to whom I might commit the bringing up of my children. That by dreams I have received help, as for other things, so in particular, how I might stay my casting of blood, and cure my dizziness, as that also that happened to thee in Cajeta, as unto Chryses when he prayed by the seashore. And when I did first apply myself to philosophy, that I did not fall into the hands of some sophists, or spent my time either in reading the manifold volumes of ordinary philosophers, nor in practising myself in the solution of arguments and fallacies, nor dwelt upon the studies of the meteors, and other natural curiosities. All these things without the assistance of the gods, and fortune, could not have been.

XV. In the country of the Quadi at Granua, these. Betimes in the morning say to thyself, This day I shalt have to do with an idle curious man, with an unthankful man, a railer, a crafty, false, or an envious man; an unsociable uncharitable man. All these ill qualities have happened unto them, through ignorance of that which is truly good and truly bad. But I that understand the nature of that which is good, that it only is to be desired, and of that which is bad, that it only is truly odious and shameful: who know moreover, that this transgressor, whosoever he be, is my kinsman, not by the same blood and seed, but by participation of the same reason, and of the same divine particle; How can I either be hurt by any of those, since it is not in their power to make me incur anything that is truly reproachful? or angry, and ill affected towards him, who by nature is so near unto me? for we are all born to be fellow-workers, as the feet, the hands, and the eyelids; as the rows of the upper and under teeth: for such therefore to be in opposition, is against nature; and what is it to chafe at, and to be averse from, but to be in opposition?

XVI. Whatsoever I am, is either flesh, or life, or that which we commonly call the mistress and overruling part of man; reason. Away with thy books, suffer not thy mind any more to be distracted, and carried to and fro; for it will not be; but as even now ready to die, think little of thy flesh: blood, bones, and a skin; a pretty piece of knit and twisted work, consisting of nerves, veins and arteries; think no more of it, than so. And as for thy life, consider what it is; a wind; not one constant wind neither, but every moment of an hour let out, and sucked in again. The third, is thy ruling part; and here consider; Thou art an old man; suffer not that excellent part to be brought in subjection, and to become slavish: suffer it not to be drawn up and down with unreasonable and unsociable lusts and motions, as it were with wires and nerves; suffer it not any more, either to repine at anything now present, or to fear and fly anything to come, which the destiny hath appointed thee.

XVII. Whatsoever proceeds from the gods immediately, that any man will grant totally depends from their divine providence. As for those things that are commonly said to happen by fortune, even those must be conceived to have dependence from nature, or from that first and general connection, and concatenation of all those things, which more apparently by the divine providence are administered and brought to pass. All things flow from thence: and whatsoever it is that is, is both necessary, and conducing to the whole (part of which thou art), and whatsoever it is that is requisite and necessary for the preservation of the general, must of necessity for every particular nature, be good and behoveful. And as for the whole, it is preserved, as by the perpetual mutation and conversion of the simple elements one into another, so also by the mutation, and alteration of things mixed and compounded. Let these things suffice thee; let them be always unto thee, as thy general rules and precepts. As for thy thirst after books, away with it with all speed, that thou die not murmuring and complaining, but truly meek and well satisfied, and from thy heart thankful unto the gods.

THE SECOND BOOK

I. Remember how long thou hast already put off these things, and how often a certain day and hour as it were, having been set unto thee by the gods, thou hast neglected it. It is high time for thee to understand the true nature both of the world, whereof thou art a part; and of that Lord and Governor of the world, from whom, as a channel from the spring, thou thyself didst flow: and that there is but a certain limit of time appointed unto thee, which if thou shalt not make use of to calm and allay the many distempers of thy soul, it will pass away and thou with it, and never after return.

II. Let it be thy earnest and incessant care as a Roman and a man to perform whatsoever it is that thou art about, with true and unfeigned gravity, natural affection, freedom and justice: and as for all other cares, and imaginations, how thou mayest ease thy mind of them. Which thou shalt do; if thou shalt go about every action as thy last action, free from all vanity, all passionate and wilful aberration from reason, and from all hypocrisy, and self-love, and dislike of those things, which by the fates or appointment of God have happened unto thee. Thou seest that those things, which for a man to hold on in a prosperous course, and to live a divine life, are requisite and necessary, are not many, for the gods will require no more of any man, that shall but keep and observe these things.

III. Do, soul, do; abuse and contemn thyself; yet a while and the time for thee to respect thyself, will be at an end. Every man's happiness depends from himself, but behold thy life is almost at an end, whiles affording thyself no respect, thou dost make thy happiness to consist in the souls, and conceits of other men.

IV. Why should any of these things that happen externally, so much distract thee? Give thyself leisure to learn some good thing, and cease roving and wandering to and fro. Thou must also take heed of another kind of wandering, for they are idle in their actions, who toil and labour in this life, and have no certain scope to which to direct all their motions, and desires.

V. For not observing the state of another man's soul, scarce was ever any man known to be unhappy. Tell whosoever they be that intend not, and guide not by reason and discretion the motions of their own souls, they must of necessity be unhappy.

VI. These things thou must always have in mind: What is the nature of the universe, and what is mine—in particular: This unto that what relation it hath: what kind of part, of what kind of universe it is: And that there is nobody that can hinder thee, but that thou mayest always both do and speak those things which are agreeable to that nature, whereof thou art a part.

VII. Theophrastus, where he compares sin with sin (as after a vulgar sense such things I grant may be compared:) says well and like a philosopher, that those sins are greater which are committed through lust, than those which are committed through anger. For he that is angry seems with a kind of grief and close contraction of himself, to turn away from reason; but he that sins through lust, being overcome by pleasure, doth in his very sin bewray a more impotent, and unmanlike disposition. Well then and like a philosopher doth he say, that he of the two is the more to be condemned, that sins with pleasure, than he that sins with grief. For indeed this latter may seem first to have been wronged, and so in some manner through grief thereof to have been forced to be angry, whereas he who through lust doth commit anything, did of himself merely resolve upon that action.

VIII. Whatsoever thou dost affect, whatsoever thou dost project, so do, and so project all, as one who, for aught thou knowest, may at this very present depart out of this life. And as for death, if there be any gods, it is no grievous thing to leave the society of men. The gods will do thee no hurt, thou mayest be sure. But if it be so that there be no gods, or that they take no care of the world, why should I desire to live in a world void of gods, and of all divine providence? But gods there be certainly, and they take care for the world; and as for those things which be truly evil, as vice and wickedness, such things they have put in a man's own power, that he might avoid them if he would: and had there been anything besides that had been truly bad and evil, they would have had a care of that also, that a man might have avoided it. But why should that be thought to hurt and prejudice a man's life in this world, which cannot any ways make man himself the better, or the worse in his own person? Neither must we think that the nature of the universe did either through ignorance pass these things, or if not as ignorant of them, yet as unable either to prevent, or better to order and dispose them. It cannot be that she through want either of power or skill, should have committed such a thing, so as to suffer all things both good and bad, equally and promiscuously, to happen unto all both good and bad. As for life therefore, and death, honour and dishonour, labour and pleasure, riches and poverty, all these things happen unto men indeed, both good and bad, equally; but as things which of themselves are neither good nor bad; because of themselves, neither shameful nor praiseworthy.

IX. Consider how quickly all things are dissolved and resolved: the bodies and substances themselves, into the matter and substance of the world: and their memories into the general age and time of the world. Consider the nature of all worldly sensible things; of those especially, which either ensnare by pleasure, or for their irksomeness are dreadful, or for their outward lustre and show are in great esteem and request, how vile and contemptible, how base and corruptible, how destitute of all true life and being they are.

X. It is the part of a man endowed with a good understanding faculty, to consider what they themselves are in very deed, from whose bare conceits and voices, honour and credit do proceed: as also what it is to die, and how if a man shall consider this by itself alone, to die, and separate from it in his mind all those things which with it usually represent themselves unto us, he can conceive of it no otherwise, than as of a work of nature, and he that fears any work of nature, is a very child. Now death, it is not only a work of nature, but also conducing to nature.

XI. Consider with thyself how man, and by what part of his, is joined unto God, and how that part of man is affected, when it is said to be diffused. There is nothing more wretched than that soul, which in a kind of circuit compasseth all things, searching (as he saith) even the very depths of the earth; and by all signs and conjectures prying into the very thoughts of other men's souls; and yet of this, is not sensible, that it is sufficient for a man to apply himself wholly, and to confine all his thoughts and cares to the tendance of that spirit which is within him, and truly and really to serve him. His service doth consist in this, that a man keep himself pure from all violent passion and evil affection, from all rashness and vanity, and from all manner of discontent, either in regard of the gods or men. For indeed whatsoever proceeds from the gods, deserves respect for their worth and excellency; and whatsoever proceeds from men, as they are our kinsmen, should by us be entertained, with love, always; sometimes, as proceeding from their ignorance, of that which is truly good and bad, (a blindness no less, than that by which we are not able to discern between white and black:) with a kind of pity and compassion also.

XII. If thou shouldst live three thousand, or as many as ten thousands of years, yet remember this, that man can part with no life properly, save with that little part of life, which he now lives: and that which he lives, is no other, than that which at every instant he parts with. That then which is longest of duration, and that which is shortest, come both to one effect. For although in regard of that which is already past there may be some inequality, yet that time which is now present and in being, is equal unto all men. And that being it which we part with whensoever we die, it doth manifestly appear, that it can be but a moment of time, that we then part with. For as for that which is either past or to come, a man cannot be said properly to part with it. For how should a man part with that which he hath not? These two things therefore thou must remember. First, that all things in the world from all eternity, by a perpetual revolution of the same times and things ever continued and renewed, are of one kind and nature; so that whether for a hundred or two hundred years only, or for an infinite space of time, a man see those things which are still the same, it can be no matter of great moment. And secondly, that that life which any the longest liver, or the shortest liver parts with, is for length and duration the very same, for that only which is present, is that, which either of them can lose, as being that only which they have; for that which he hath not, no man can truly be said to lose.

XIII. Remember that all is but opinion and conceit, for those things are plain and apparent, which were spoken unto Monimus the Cynic; and as plain and apparent is the use that may be made of those things, if that which is true and serious in them, be received as well as that which is sweet and pleasing.

XIV. A man's soul doth wrong and disrespect itself first and especially, when as much as in itself lies it becomes an aposteme, and as it were an excrescency of the world, for to be grieved and displeased with anything that happens in the world, is direct apostacy from the nature of the universe; part of which, all particular natures of the world, are. Secondly, when she either is averse from any man, or led by contrary desires or affections, tending to his hurt and prejudice; such as are the souls of them that are angry. Thirdly, when she is overcome by any pleasure or pain. Fourthly, when she doth dissemble, and covertly and falsely either doth or saith anything. Fifthly, when she doth either affect or endeavour anything to no certain end, but rashly and without due ratiocination and consideration, how consequent or inconsequent it is to the common end. For even the least things ought not to be done, without relation unto the end; and the end of the reasonable creatures is, to follow and obey him, who is the reason as it were, and the law of this great city, and ancient commonwealth.

XV. The time of a man's life is as a point; the substance of it ever flowing, the sense obscure; and the whole composition of the body tending to corruption. His soul is restless, fortune uncertain, and fame doubtful; to be brief, as a stream so are all things belonging to the body; as a dream, or as a smoke, so are all that belong unto the soul. Our life is a warfare, and a mere pilgrimage. Fame after life is no better than oblivion. What is it then that will adhere and follow? Only one thing, philosophy. And philosophy doth consist in this, for a man to preserve that spirit which is within him, from all manner of contumelies and injuries, and above all pains or pleasures; never to do anything either rashly, or feignedly, or hypocritically: wholly to depend from himself and his own proper actions: all things that happen unto him to embrace contentedly, as coming from Him from whom he himself also came; and above all things, with all meekness and a calm cheerfulness, to expect death, as being nothing else but the resolution of those elements, of which every creature is composed. And if the elements themselves suffer nothing by this their perpetual conversion of one into another, that dissolution, and alteration, which is so common unto all, why should it be feared by any? Is not this according to nature? But nothing that is according to nature can be evil.

Whilst I was at Carnuntum.

THE THIRD BOOK

I. A man must not only consider how daily his life wasteth and decreaseth, but this also, that if he live long, he cannot be certain, whether his understanding shall continue so able and sufficient, for either discreet consideration, in matter of businesses; or for contemplation: it being the thing, whereon true knowledge of things both divine and human, doth depend. For if once he shall begin to dote, his respiration, nutrition, his imaginative, and appetitive, and other natural faculties, may still continue the same: he shall find no want of them. But how to make that right use of himself that he should, how to observe exactly in all things that which is right and just, how to redress and rectify all wrong, or sudden apprehensions and imaginations, and even of this particular, whether he should live any longer or no, to consider duly; for all such things, wherein the best strength and vigour of the mind is most requisite; his power and ability will be past and gone. Thou must hasten therefore; not only because thou art every day nearer unto death than other, but also because that intellective faculty in thee, whereby thou art enabled to know the true nature of things, and to order all thy actions by that knowledge, doth daily waste and decay: or, may fail thee before thou die.

II. This also thou must observe, that whatsoever it is that naturally doth happen to things natural, hath somewhat in itself that is pleasing and delightful: as a great loaf when it is baked, some parts of it cleave as it were, and part asunder, and make the crust of it rugged and unequal, and yet those parts of it, though in some sort it be against the art and intention of baking itself, that they are thus cleft and parted, which should have been and were first made all even and uniform, they become it well nevertheless, and have a certain peculiar property, to stir the appetite. So figs are accounted fairest and ripest then, when they begin to shrink, and wither as it were. So ripe olives, when they are next to putrefaction, then are they in their proper beauty. The hanging down of grapes—the brow of a lion, the froth of a foaming wild boar, and many other like things, though by themselves considered, they are far from any beauty, yet because they happen naturally, they both are comely, and delightful; so that if a man shall with a profound mind and apprehension, consider all things in the world, even among all those things which are but mere accessories and natural appendices as it were, there will scarce appear anything unto him, wherein he will not find matter of pleasure and delight. So will he behold with as much pleasure the true *rictus* of wild beasts, as those which by skilful painters and other artificers are imitated. So will he be able to perceive the proper ripeness and beauty of old age, whether in man or woman: and whatsoever else it is that is beautiful and alluring in whatsoever is, with chaste and continent eyes he will soon find out and discern. Those and many other things will he discern, not credible unto every one, but unto them only who are truly and familiarly acquainted, both with nature itself, and all natural things.

III. Hippocrates having cured many sicknesses, fell sick himself and died. The Chaldeans and Astrologians having foretold the deaths of divers, were afterwards themselves surprised by the fates. Alexander and Pompeius, and Caius Cæsar, having destroyed so many towns, and cut off in the field so many thousands both of horse and foot, yet they themselves at last were fain to part with their own lives. Heraclitus having written so many natural tracts concerning the last and general conflagration of the world, died afterwards all filled with water within, and all bedaubed with dirt and dung without. Lice killed Democritus; and Socrates, another sort of vermin, wicked ungodly men. How then stands the case? Thou hast taken ship, thou hast sailed, thou art come to land, go out, if to another life, there also shalt thou find gods, who are everywhere. If all life and sense shall cease, then shalt thou cease also to be subject to either pains or pleasures; and to serve and tend this vile cottage; so much the viler, by how much that which ministers unto it doth excel; the one being a rational substance, and a spirit, the other nothing but earth and blood.

IV. Spend not the remnant of thy days in thoughts and fancies concerning other men, when it is not in relation to some common good, when by it thou art hindered from some other better work. That is, spend not thy time in thinking, what such a man doth, and to what end: what he saith, and what he thinks, and what he is about, and such other things or curiosities, which make a man to rove and wander from the care and observation of that part of himself, which is rational, and overruling. See therefore in the whole series and connection of thy thoughts, that thou be careful to prevent whatsoever is idle and impertinent: but especially, whatsoever is curious and malicious: and thou must use thyself to think only of such things, of which if a man upon a sudden should ask thee, what it is that thou art now thinking, thou mayest answer This, and That, freely and boldly, that so by thy thoughts it may presently appear that in all thee is sincere, and peaceable; as becometh one that is made for society, and regards not pleasures, nor gives way to any voluptuous imaginations at all: free from all contentiousness, envy, and suspicion, and from whatsoever else thou wouldest blush to confess thy thoughts were set upon. He that is such, is he surely that doth not put off to lay hold on that which is best indeed, a very priest and minister of the gods, well acquainted and in good correspondence with him especially that is seated and placed within himself, as in a temple and sacrary: to whom also he keeps and preserves himself unspotted by pleasure, undaunted by pain; free from any manner of wrong, or contumely, by himself offered unto himself: not capable of any evil from others: a wrestler of the best sort, and for the highest prize, that he may not be cast down by any passion or affection of his own; deeply dyed and drenched in righteousness, embracing and accepting with his whole heart whatsoever either happeneth or is allotted unto him. One who not often, nor without some great necessity tending to some public good, mindeth what any other, either speaks, or doth, or purposeth: for those things only that are in his own power, or that are truly his own, are the objects of his employments, and his thoughts are ever taken up with those things, which of the whole universe are by the fates or Providence destinated and appropriated unto himself. Those things that are his own, and in his own power, he himself takes order, for that they be good: and as for those that happen unto him, he believes them to be so. For that lot and portion which is assigned to every one, as it is unavoidable and necessary, so is it always profitable. He remembers besides that whatsoever partakes of reason, is akin unto him, and that to care for all men generally, is agreeing to the nature of a man: but as for honour and praise, that they ought not generally to be admitted and accepted of from all, but from such only, who live according to nature. As for them that do not, what manner of men they be at home, or abroad; day or night, how conditioned themselves with what manner of conditions, or with men of what conditions they moil and pass away the time together, he knoweth, and remembers right well, he therefore regards not such praise and approbation, as proceeding from them, who cannot like and approve themselves.

V. Do nothing against thy will, nor contrary to the community, nor without due examination, nor with reluctancy. Affect not to set out thy thoughts with curious neat language. Be neither a great talker, nor a great undertaker. Moreover, let thy God that is in thee to rule over thee, find by thee, that he hath to do with a man; an aged man; a sociable man; a Roman; a prince; one that hath ordered his life, as one that expecteth, as it were, nothing but the sound of the trumpet, sounding a retreat to depart out of this life with all expedition. One who for his word or actions neither needs an oath, nor any man to be a witness.

VI. To be cheerful, and to stand in no need, either of other men's help or attendance, or of that rest and tranquillity, which thou must be beholding to others for. Rather like one that is straight of himself, or hath ever been straight, than one that hath been rectified.

VII. If thou shalt find anything in this mortal life better than righteousness, than truth, temperance, fortitude, and in general better than a mind contented both with those things which according to right and reason she doth, and in those, which without her will and knowledge happen unto thee by the providence; if I say, thou canst find out anything better than this, apply thyself unto it with thy whole heart, and that which is best wheresoever thou dost find it, enjoy freely. But if nothing thou shalt find worthy to be preferred to that spirit which is within thee; if nothing better than to subject unto thee thine own lusts and desires, and not to give way to any fancies or imaginations before thou hast duly considered of them, nothing better than to withdraw thyself (to use Socrates his words) from all sensuality, and submit thyself unto the gods, and to have care of all men in general: if thou shalt find that all other things in comparison of this, are but vile, and of little moment; then give not way to any other thing, which being once though but affected and inclined unto, it will no more be in thy power without all distraction as thou oughtest to prefer and to pursue after that good, which is thine own and thy proper good. For it is not lawful, that anything that is of another and inferior kind and nature, be it what it will, as either popular applause, or honour, or riches, or pleasures; should be suffered to confront and contest as it were, with that which is rational, and operatively good. For all these things, if once though but for a while, they begin to please, they presently prevail, and pervert a man's mind, or turn a man from the right way. Do thou therefore I say absolutely and freely make choice of that which is best, and stick unto it. Now, that they say is best, which is most profitable. If they mean profitable to man as he is a rational man, stand thou to it, and maintain it; but if they mean profitable, as he is a creature, only reject it; and from this thy tenet and conclusion keep off carefully all plausible shows and colours of external appearance, that thou mayest be able to discern things rightly.

VIII. Never esteem of anything as profitable, which shall ever constrain thee either to break thy faith, or to lose thy modesty; to hate any man, to suspect, to curse, to dissemble, to lust after anything, that requireth the secret of walls or veils. But he that preferreth before all things his rational part and spirit, and the sacred mysteries of virtue which issueth from it, he shall never lament and exclaim, never sigh; he shall never want either solitude or company: and which is chiefest of all, he shall live without either desire or fear. And as for life, whether for a long or short time he shall enjoy his soul thus compassed about with a body, he is altogether indifferent. For if even now he were to depart, he is as ready for it, as for any other action, which may be performed with modesty and decency. For all his life long, this is his only care, that his mind may always be occupied in such intentions and objects, as are proper to a rational sociable creature.

IX. In the mind that is once truly disciplined and purged, thou canst not find anything, either foul or impure, or as it were festered: nothing that is either servile, or affected: no partial tie; no malicious averseness; nothing obnoxious; nothing concealed. The life of such an one, death can never surprise as imperfect; as of an actor, that should die before he had ended, or the play itself were at an end, a man might speak.

X. Use thine opinative faculty with all honour and respect, for in her indeed is all: that thy opinion do not beget in thy understanding anything contrary to either nature, or the proper constitution of a rational creature. The end and object of a rational constitution is, to do nothing rashly, to be kindly affected towards men, and in all things willingly to submit unto the gods. Casting therefore all other things aside, keep thyself to these few, and remember withal that no man properly can be said to live more than that which is now present, which is but a moment of time. Whatsoever is besides either is already past, or uncertain. The time therefore that any man doth live, is but a little, and the place where he liveth, is but a very little corner of the earth, and the greatest fame that can remain of a man after his death, even that is but little, and that too, such as it is whilst it is, is by the succession of silly mortal men preserved, who likewise shall shortly die, and even whiles they live know not what in very deed they themselves are: and much less can know one, who long before is dead and gone.

XI. To these ever-present helps and mementoes, let one more be added, ever to make a particular description and delineation as it were of every object that presents itself to thy mind, that thou mayest wholly and throughly contemplate it, in its own proper nature, bare and naked; wholly, and severally; divided into its several parts and quarters: and then by thyself in thy mind, to call both it, and those things of which it doth consist, and in which it shall be resolved, by their own proper true names, and appellations. For there is nothing so effectual to beget true magnanimity, as to be able truly and methodically to examine and consider all things that happen in this life, and so to penetrate into their natures, that at the same time, this also may concur in our apprehensions: what is the true use of it? and what is the true nature of this universe, to which it is useful? how much in regard of the universe may it be esteemed? how much in regard of man, a citizen of the supreme city, of which all other cities in the world are as it were but houses and families?

XII. What is this, that now my fancy is set upon? of what things doth it consist? how long can it last? which of all the virtues is the proper virtue for this present use? as whether meekness, fortitude, truth, faith, sincerity, contentation, or any of the rest? Of everything therefore thou must use thyself to say, This immediately comes from God, this by that fatal connection, and concatenation of things, or (which almost comes to one) by some coincidental casualty. And as for this, it proceeds from my neighbour, my kinsman, my fellow: through his ignorance indeed, because he knows not what is truly natural unto him: but I know it, and therefore carry myself towards him according to the natural law of fellowship; that is kindly, and justly. As for those things that of themselves are altogether indifferent, as in my best judgment I conceive everything to deserve more or less, so I carry myself towards it.

XIII. If thou shalt intend that which is present, following the rule of right and reason carefully, solidly, meekly, and shalt not intermix any other businesses, but shall study this only to preserve thy spirit unpolluted, and pure, and shall cleave unto him without either hope or fear of anything, in all things that thou shalt either do or speak, contenting thyself with heroical truth, thou shalt live happily; and from this, there is no man that can hinder thee.

XIV. As physicians and chirurgeons have always their instruments ready at hand for all sudden cures; so have thou always thy dogmata in a readiness for the knowledge of things, both divine and human: and whatsoever thou dost, even in the smallest things that thou dost, thou must ever remember that mutual relation, and connection that is between these two things divine, and things human. For without relation unto God, thou shalt never speed in any worldly actions; nor on the other side in any divine, without some respect had to things human.

XV. Be not deceived; for thou shalt never live to read thy moral commentaries, nor the acts of the famous Romans and Grecians; nor those excerpta from several books; all which thou hadst provided and laid up for thyself against thine old age. Hasten therefore to an end, and giving over all vain hopes, help thyself in time if thou carest for thyself, as thou oughtest to do.

XVI. To steal, to sow, to buy, to be at rest, to see what is to be done (which is not seen by the eyes, but by another kind of sight:) what these words mean, and how many ways to be understood, they do not understand. The body, the soul, the understanding. As the senses naturally belong to the body, and the desires and affections to the soul, so do the dogmata to the understanding.

XVII. To be capable of fancies and imaginations, is common to man and beast. To be violently drawn and moved by the lusts and desires of the soul, is proper to wild beasts and monsters, such as Phalaris and Nero were. To follow reason for ordinary duties and actions is common to them also, who believe not that there be any gods, and for their advantage would make no conscience to betray their own country; and who when once the doors be shut upon them, dare do anything. If therefore all things else be common to these likewise, it follows, that for a man to like and embrace all things that happen and are destinated unto him, and not to trouble and molest that spirit which is seated in the temple of his own breast, with a multitude of vain fancies and imaginations, but to keep him propitious and to obey him as a god, never either speaking anything contrary to truth, or doing anything contrary to justice, is the only true property of a good man. And such a one, though no man should believe that he liveth as he doth, either sincerely and conscionably, or cheerful and contentedly; yet is he neither with any man at all angry for it, nor diverted by it from the way that leadeth to the end of his life, through which a man must pass pure, ever ready to depart, and willing of himself without any compulsion to fit and accommodate himself to his proper lot and portion.

THE FOURTH BOOK

I. That inward mistress part of man if it be in its own true natural temper, is towards all worldly chances and events ever so disposed and affected, that it will easily turn and apply itself to that which may be, and is within its own power to compass, when that cannot be which at first it intended. For it never doth absolutely addict and apply itself to any one object, but whatsoever it is that it doth now intend and prosecute, it doth prosecute it with exception and reservation; so that whatsoever it is that falls out contrary to its first intentions, even that afterwards it makes its proper object. Even as the fire when it prevails upon those things that are in his way; by which things indeed a little fire would have been quenched, but a great fire doth soon turn to its own nature, and so consume whatsoever comes in his way: yea by those very things it is made greater and greater.

II. Let nothing be done rashly, and at random, but all things according to the most exact and perfect rules of art.

III. They seek for themselves private retiring places, as country villages, the sea-shore, mountains; yea thou thyself art wont to long much after such places. But all this thou must know proceeds from simplicity in the highest degree. At what time soever thou wilt, it is in thy power to retire into thyself, and to be at rest, and free from all businesses. A man cannot any whither retire better than to his own soul; he especially who is beforehand provided of such things within, which whensoever he doth withdraw himself to look in, may presently afford unto him perfect ease and tranquillity. By tranquillity I understand a decent orderly disposition and carriage, free from all confusion and tumultuousness. Afford then thyself this retiring continually, and thereby refresh and renew thyself. Let these precepts be brief and fundamental, which as soon as thou dost call them to mind, may suffice thee to purge thy soul throughly, and to send thee away well pleased with those things whatsoever they be, which now again after this short withdrawing of thy soul into herself thou dost return unto. For what is it that thou art offended at? Can it be at the wickedness of men, when thou dost call to mind this conclusion, that all reasonable creatures are made one for another? and that it is part of justice to bear with them? and that it is against their wills that they offend? and how many already, who once likewise prosecuted their enmities, suspected, hated, and fiercely contended, are now long ago stretched out, and reduced unto ashes? It is time for thee to make an end. As for those things which among the common chances of the world happen unto thee as thy particular lot and portion, canst thou be displeased with any of them, when thou dost call that our ordinary dilemma to mind, either a providence, or Democritus his atoms; and with it, whatsoever we brought to prove that the whole world is as it were one city? And as for thy body, what canst thou fear, if thou dost consider that thy mind and understanding, when once it hath recollected itself, and knows its own power, hath in this life and breath (whether it run smoothly and gently, or whether harshly and rudely), no interest at all, but is altogether indifferent: and whatsoever else thou hast heard and assented unto concerning either pain or pleasure? But the care of thine honour and reputation will perchance distract thee? How can that be, if thou dost look back, and consider both how quickly all things that are, are forgotten, and what an immense chaos of eternity was before, and will follow after all things: and the vanity of praise, and the inconstancy and variableness of human judgments and opinions, and the narrowness of the place, wherein it is limited and circumscribed? For the whole earth is but as one point; and of it, this inhabited part of it, is but a very little part; and of this part, how many in number, and what manner of men are they, that will commend thee? What remains then, but that thou often put in practice this kind of retiring of thyself, to this little part of thyself; and above all things, keep thyself from distraction, and intend not anything vehemently, but be free and consider all things, as a man whose proper object is Virtue, as a man whose true nature is to be kind and sociable, as a citizen, as a mortal creature. Among other things, which to consider, and look into thou must use to withdraw thyself, let those two be among the most obvious and at hand. One, that the things or objects themselves reach not unto the soul, but stand without still and quiet, and that it is from the opinion only which is within, that all the tumult and all the trouble doth proceed. The next, that all these things, which now thou seest, shall within a very little while be changed, and be no more: and ever call to mind, how many changes and alterations in the world thou thyself hast already been an eyewitness of in thy time. This world is mere change, and this life, opinion.

IV. If to understand and to be reasonable be common unto all men, then is that reason, for which we are termed reasonable, common unto all. If reason is general, then is that reason also, which prescribeth what is to be done and what not, common unto all. If that, then law. If law, then are we fellow-citizens. If so, then are we partners in some one commonweal. If so, then the world is as it were a city. For which other commonweal is it, that all men can be said to be members of? From this common city it is, that understanding, reason, and law is derived unto us, for from whence else? For as that which in me is earthly I have from some common earth; and that which is moist from some other element is imparted; as my breath and life hath its proper fountain; and that likewise which is dry and fiery in me: (for there is nothing which doth not proceed from something; as also there is nothing that can be reduced unto mere nothing:) so also is there some common beginning from whence my understanding hath proceeded.

V. As generation is, so also death, a secret of nature's wisdom: a mixture of elements, resolved into the same elements again, a thing surely which no man ought to be ashamed of: in a series of other fatal events and consequences, which a rational creature is subject unto, not improper or incongruous, nor contrary to the natural and proper constitution of man himself.

VI. Such and such things, from such and such causes, must of necessity proceed. He that would not have such things to happen, is as he that would have the fig-tree grow without any sap or moisture. In sum, remember this, that within a very little while, both thou and he shall both be dead, and after a little while more, not so much as your names and memories shall be remaining.

VII. Let opinion be taken away, and no man will think himself wronged. If no man shall think himself wronged, then is there no more any such thing as wrong. That which makes not man himself the worse, cannot make his life the worse, neither can it hurt him either inwardly or outwardly. It was expedient in nature that it should be so, and therefore necessary.

VIII. Whatsoever doth happen in the world, doth happen justly, and so if thou dost well take heed, thou shalt find it. I say not only in right order by a series of inevitable consequences, but according to justice and as it were by way of equal distribution, according to the true worth of everything. Continue then to take notice of it, as thou hast begun, and whatsoever thou dost, do it not without this proviso, that it be a thing of that nature that a good man (as the word good is properly taken) may do it. This observe carefully in every action.

IX. Conceit no such things, as he that wrongeth thee conceiveth, or would have thee to conceive, but look into the matter itself, and see what it is in very truth.

X. These two rules, thou must have always in a readiness. First, do nothing at all, but what reason proceeding from that regal and supreme part, shall for the good and benefit of men, suggest unto thee. And secondly, if any man that is present shall be able to rectify thee or to turn thee from some erroneous persuasion, that thou be always ready to change thy mind, and this change to proceed, not from any respect of any pleasure or credit thereon depending, but always from some probable apparent ground of justice, or of some public good thereby to be furthered; or from some other such inducement.

XI. Hast thou reason? I have. Why then makest thou not use of it? For if thy reason do her part, what more canst thou require?

XII. As a part hitherto thou hast had a particular subsistence: and now shalt thou vanish away into the common substance of Him, who first begot thee, or rather thou shalt be resumed again into that original rational substance, out of which all others have issued, and are propagated. Many small pieces of frankincense are set upon the same altar, one drops first and is consumed, another after; and it comes all to one.

XIII. Within ten days, if so happen, thou shalt be esteemed a god of them, who now if thou shalt return to the dogmata and to the honouring of reason, will esteem of thee no better than of a mere brute, and of an ape.

XIV. Not as though thou hadst thousands of years to live. Death hangs over thee: whilst yet thou livest, whilst thou mayest, be good.

XV. Now much time and leisure doth he gain, who is not curious to know what his neighbour hath said, or hath done, or hath attempted, but only what he doth himself, that it may be just and holy? or to express it in Agathos' words, Not to look about upon the evil conditions of others, but to run on straight in the line, without any loose and extravagant agitation.

XVI. He who is greedy of credit and reputation after his death, doth not consider, that they themselves by whom he is remembered, shall soon after every one of them be dead; and they likewise that succeed those; until at last all memory, which hitherto by the succession of men admiring and soon after dying hath had its course, be quite extinct. But suppose that both they that shall remember thee, and thy memory with them should be immortal, what is that to thee? I will not say to thee after thou art dead; but even to thee living, what is thy praise? But only for a secret and politic consideration, which we call οἰκονομίαν, or dispensation. For as for that, that it is the gift of nature, whatsoever is commended in thee, what might be objected from thence, let that now that we are upon another consideration be omitted as unseasonable. That which is fair and goodly, whatsoever it be, and in what respect soever it be, that it is fair and goodly, it is so of itself, and terminates in itself, not admitting praise as a part or member: that therefore which is praised, is not thereby made either better or worse. This I understand even of those things, that are commonly called fair and good, as those which are commended either for the matter itself, or for curious workmanship. As for that which is truly good, what can it stand in need of more than either justice or truth; or more than either kindness and modesty? Which of all those, either becomes good or fair, because commended; or dispraised suffers any damage? Doth the emerald become worse in itself, or more vile if it be not commended? Doth gold, or ivory, or purple? Is there anything that doth though never so common, as a knife, a flower, or a tree?

XVII. If so be that the souls remain after death (say they that will not believe it); how is the air from all eternity able to contain them? How is the earth (say I) ever from that time able to Contain the bodies of them that are buried? For as here the change and resolution of dead bodies into another kind of subsistence (whatsoever it be;) makes place for other dead bodies: so the souls after death transferred into the air, after they have conversed there a while, are either by way of transmutation, or transfusion, or conflagration, received again into that original rational substance, from which all others do proceed: and so give way to those souls, who before coupled and associated unto bodies, now begin to subsist single. This, upon a supposition that the souls after death do for a while subsist single, may be answered. And here, (besides the number of bodies, so buried and contained by the earth), we may further consider the number of several beasts, eaten by us men, and by other creatures. For notwithstanding that such a multitude of them is daily consumed, and as it were buried in the bodies of the eaters, yet is the same place and body able to contain them, by reason of their conversion, partly into blood, partly into air and fire. What in these things is the speculation of truth? to divide things into that which is passive and material; and that which is active and formal.

XVIII. Not to wander out of the way, but upon every motion and desire, to perform that which is just: and ever to be careful to attain to the true natural apprehension of every fancy, that presents itself.

XIX. Whatsoever is expedient unto thee, O World, is expedient unto me; nothing can either be 'unseasonable unto me, or out of date, which unto thee is seasonable. Whatsoever thy seasons bear, shall ever by me be esteemed as happy fruit, and increase. O Nature! from thee are all things, in thee all things subsist, and to thee all tend. Could he say of Athens, Thou lovely city of Cecrops; and shalt not thou say of the world, Thou lovely city of God?

XX. They will say commonly, Meddle not with many things, if thou wilt live cheerfully. Certainly there is nothing better, than for a man to confine himself to necessary actions; to such and so many only, as reason in a creature that knows itself born for society, will command and enjoin. This will not only procure that cheerfulness, which from the goodness, but that also, which from the paucity of actions doth usually proceed. For since it is so, that most of those things, which we either speak or do, are unnecessary; if a man shall cut them off, it must needs follow that he shall thereby gain much leisure, and save much trouble, and therefore at every action a man must privately by way of admonition suggest unto himself, What? may not this that now I go about, be of the number of unnecessary actions? Neither must he use himself to cut off actions only, but thoughts and imaginations also, that are unnecessary for so will unnecessary consequent actions the better be prevented and cut off.

XXI. Try also how a good man's life; (of one, who is well pleased with those things whatsoever, which among the common changes and chances of this world fall to his own lot and share; and can live well contented and fully satisfied in the justice of his own proper present action, and in the goodness of his disposition for the future:) will agree with thee. Thou hast had experience of that other kind of life: make now trial of this also. Trouble not thyself any more henceforth, reduce thyself unto perfect simplicity. Doth any man offend? It is against himself that he doth offend: why should it trouble thee? Hath anything happened unto thee? It is well, whatsoever it be, it is that which of all the common chances of the world from the very beginning in the series of all other things that have, or shall happen, was destinated and appointed unto thee. To comprehend all in a few words, our life is short; we must endeavour to gain the present time with best discretion and justice. Use recreation with sobriety.

XXII. Either this world is a κόσμος, or comely piece, because all disposed and governed by certain order: or if it be a mixture, though confused, yet still it is a comely piece. For is it possible that in thee there should be any beauty at all, and that in the whole world there should be nothing but disorder and confusion? and all things in it too, by natural different properties one from another differenced and distinguished; and yet all through diffused, and by natural sympathy, one to another united, as they are?

XXIII. A black or malign disposition, an effeminate disposition; an hard inexorable disposition, a wild inhuman disposition, a sheepish disposition, a childish disposition; a blockish, a false, a scurril, a fraudulent, a tyrannical: what then? If he be a stranger in the world, that knows not the things that are in it; why not be a stranger as well, that wonders at the things that are done in it?

XXIV. He is a true fugitive, that flies from reason, by which men are sociable. He blind, who cannot see with the eyes of his understanding. He poor, that stands in need of another, and hath not in himself all things needful for this life. He an aposteme of the world, who by being discontented with those things that happen unto him in the world, doth as it were apostatise, and separate himself from common nature's rational administration. For the same nature it is that brings this unto thee, whatsoever it be, that first brought thee into the world. He raises sedition in the city, who by irrational actions withdraws his own soul from that one and common soul of all rational creatures.

XXV. There is, who without so much as a coat; and there is, who without so much as a book, doth put philosophy in practice. I am half naked, neither have I bread to eat, and yet I depart not from reason, saith one. But I say; I want the food of good teaching, and instructions, and yet I depart not from reason.

XXVI. What art and profession soever thou hast learned, endeavour to affect it, and comfort thyself in it; and pass the remainder of thy life as one who from his whole heart commits himself and whatsoever belongs unto him, unto the gods: and as for men, carry not thyself either tyrannically or servilely towards any.

XXVII. Consider in my mind, for example's sake, the times of Vespasian: thou shalt see but the same things: some marrying, some bringing up children, some sick, some dying, some fighting, some feasting, some merchandising, some tilling, some flattering, some boasting, some suspecting, some undermining, some wishing to die, some fretting and murmuring at their present estate, some wooing, some hoarding, some seeking after magistracies, and some after kingdoms. And is not that their age quite over, and ended? Again, consider now the times of Trajan. There likewise thou seest the very self-same things, and that age also is now over and ended. In the like manner consider other periods, both of times and of whole nations, and see how many men, after they had with all their might and main intended and prosecuted some one worldly thing or other did soon after drop away, and were resolved into the elements. But especially thou must call to mind them, whom thou thyself in thy lifetime hast known much distracted about vain things, and in the meantime neglecting to do that, and closely and unseparably (as fully satisfied with it) to adhere unto it, which their own proper constitution did require. And here thou must remember, that thy carriage in every business must be according to the worth and due proportion of it, for so shalt thou not easily be tired out and vexed, if thou shalt not dwell upon small matters longer than is fitting.

XXVIII. Those words which once were common and ordinary, are now become obscure and obsolete; and so the names of men once commonly known and famous, are now become in a manner obscure and obsolete names. Camillus, Cæso, Volesius, Leonnatus; not long after, Scipio, Cato, then Augustus, then Adrianus, then Antoninus Pius: all these in a short time will be out of date, and, as things of another world as it were, become fabulous. And this I say of them, who once shined as the wonders of their ages, for as for the rest, no sooner are they expired, than with them all their fame and memory. And what is it then that shall always be remembered? all is vanity. What is it that we must bestow our care and diligence upon? even upon this only: that our minds and wills be just; that our actions be charitable; that our speech be never deceitful, or that our understanding be not subject to error; that our inclination be always set to embrace whatsoever shall happen unto us, as necessary, as usual, as ordinary, as flowing from such a beginning, and such a fountain, from which both thou thyself and all things are. Willingly therefore, and wholly surrender up thyself unto that fatal concatenation, yielding up thyself unto the fates, to be disposed of at their pleasure.

XXIX. Whatsoever is now present, and from day to day hath its existence; all objects of memories, and the minds and memories themselves, incessantly consider, all things that are, have their being by change and alteration.

Use thyself therefore often to meditate upon this, that the nature of the universe delights in nothing more, than in altering those things that are, and in making others like unto them. So that we may say, that whatsoever is, is but as it were the seed of that which shall be. For if thou think that that only is seed, which either the earth or the womb receiveth, thou art very simple.

XXX. Thou art now ready to die, and yet hast thou not attained to that perfect simplicity: thou art yet subject to many troubles and perturbations; not yet free from all fear and suspicion of external accidents; nor yet either so meekly disposed towards all men, as thou shouldest; or so affected as one, whose only study and only wisdom is, to be just in all his actions.

XXXI. Behold and observe, what is the state of their rational part; and those that the world doth account wise, see what things they fly and are afraid of; and what things they hunt after.

XXXII. In another man's mind and understanding thy evil Cannot subsist, nor in any proper temper or distemper of the natural constitution of thy body, which is but as it were the coat or cottage of thy soul. Wherein then, but in that part of thee, wherein the conceit, and apprehension of any misery can subsist? Let not that part therefore admit any such conceit, and then all is well. Though thy body which is so near it should either be cut or burnt, or suffer any corruption or putrefaction, yet let that part to which it belongs to judge of these, be still at rest; that is, let her judge this, that whatsoever it is, that equally may happen to a wicked man, and to a good man, is neither good nor evil. For that which happens equally to him that lives according to nature, and to him that doth not, is neither according to nature, nor against it; and by consequent, neither good nor bad.

XXXIII. Ever consider and think upon the world as being but one living substance, and having but one soul, and how all things in the world, are terminated into one sensitive power; and are done by one general motion as it were, and deliberation of that one soul; and how all things that are, concur in the cause of one another's being, and by what manner of connection and concatenation all things happen.

XXXIV. What art thou, that better and divine part excepted, but as Epictetus said well, a wretched soul, appointed to carry a carcass up and down?

XXXV. To suffer change can be no hurt; as no benefit it is, by change to attain to being. The age and time of the world is as it were a flood and swift current, consisting of the things that are brought to pass in the world. For as soon as anything hath appeared, and is passed away, another succeeds, and that also will presently out of sight.

XXXVI. Whatsoever doth happen in the world, is, in the course of nature, as usual and ordinary as a rose in the spring, and fruit in summer. Of the same nature is sickness and death; slander, and lying in wait, and whatsoever else ordinarily doth unto fools use to be occasion either of joy or sorrow. That, whatsoever it is, that comes after, doth always very naturally, and as it were familiarly, follow upon that which was before. For thou must consider the things of the world, not as a loose independent number, consisting merely of necessary events; but as a discreet connection of things orderly and harmoniously disposed. There is then to be seen in the things of the world, not a bare succession, but an admirable correspondence and affinity.

XXXVII. Let that of Heraclitus never be out of thy mind, that the death of earth, is water, and the death of water, is air; and the death of air, is fire; and so on the contrary. Remember him also who was ignorant whither the way did lead, and how that reason being the thing by which all things in the world are administered, and which men are continually and most inwardly conversant with: yet is the thing, which ordinarily they are most in opposition with, and how those things which daily happen among them, cease not daily to be strange unto them, and that we should not either speak, or do anything as men in their sleep, by opinion and bare imagination: for then we think we speak and do, and that we must not be as children, who follow their father's example; for best reason alleging their bare καθότι παρειλήφαμεν; or, as by successive tradition from our forefathers we have received it.

XXXVIII. Even as if any of the gods should tell thee, Thou shalt certainly die to-morrow, or next day, thou wouldst not, except thou wert extremely base and pusillanimous, take it for a great benefit, rather to die the next day after, than to-morrow; (for alas, what is the difference!) so, for the same reason, think it no great matter to die rather many years after, than the very next day.

XXXIX. Let it be thy perpetual meditation, how many physicians who once looked so grim, and so theatrically shrunk their brows upon their patients, are dead and gone themselves. How many astrologers, after that in great ostentation they had foretold the death of some others, how many philosophers after so many elaborate tracts and volumes concerning either mortality or immortality; how many brave captains and commanders, after the death and slaughter of so many; how many kings and tyrants, after they had with such horror and insolency abused their power upon men's lives, as though themselves had been immortal; how many, that I may so speak, whole cities both men and towns: Helice, Pompeii, Herculaneum, and others innumerable are dead and gone. Run them over also, whom thou thyself, one after another, hast known in thy time to drop away. Such and such a one took care of such and such a one's burial, and soon after was buried himself. So one, so another: and all things in a short time. For herein lieth all indeed, ever to look upon all worldly things, as things for their continuance, that are but for a day: and for their worth, most vile, and contemptible, as for example, What is man? That which but the other day when he was conceived was vile snivel; and within few days shall be either an embalmed carcass, or mere ashes. Thus must thou according to truth and nature, throughly consider how man's life is but for a very moment of time, and so depart meek and contented: even as if a ripe olive falling should praise the ground that bare her, and give thanks to the tree that begat her.

XL. Thou must be like a promontory of the sea, against which though the waves beat continually, yet it both itself stands, and about it are those swelling waves stilled and quieted.

XLI. Oh, wretched I, to whom this mischance is happened! nay, happy I, to whom this thing being happened, I can continue without grief; neither wounded by that which is present, nor in fear of that which is to come. For as for this, it might have happened unto any man, but any man having such a thing befallen him, could not have continued without grief. Why then should that rather be an unhappiness, than this a happiness? But however, canst thou, O man! term that unhappiness, which is no mischance to the nature of man I Canst thou think that a mischance to the nature of man, which is not contrary to the end and will of his nature? What then hast thou learned is the will of man's nature? Doth that then which hath happened unto thee, hinder thee from being just? or magnanimous? or temperate? or wise? or circumspect? or true? or modest? or free? or from anything else of all those things in the present enjoying and possession whereof the nature of man, (as then enjoying all that is proper unto her,) is fully satisfied? Now to conclude; upon all occasion of sorrow remember henceforth to make use of this dogma, that whatsoever it is that hath happened unto thee, is in very deed no such thing of itself, as a misfortune; but that to bear it generously, is certainly great happiness.

XLII. It is but an ordinary coarse one, yet it is a good effectual remedy against the fear of death, for a man to consider in his mind the examples of such, who greedily and covetously (as it were) did for a long time enjoy their lives. What have they got more, than they whose deaths have been untimely? Are not they themselves dead at the last? as Cadiciant's, Fabius, Julianus Lepidus, or any other who in their lifetime having buried many, were at the last buried themselves. The whole space of any man's life, is but little; and as little as it is, with what troubles, with what manner of dispositions, and in the society of how wretched a body must it be passed! Let it be therefore unto thee altogether as a matter of indifferency. For if thou shalt look backward; behold, what an infinite chaos of time doth present itself unto thee; and as infinite a chaos, if thou shalt look forward. In that which is so infinite, what difference can there be between that which liveth but three days, and that which liveth three ages?

XLIII. Let thy course ever be the most compendious way. The most compendious, is that which is according to nature: that is, in all both words and deeds, ever to follow that which is most sound and perfect. For such a resolution will free a man from all trouble, strife, dissembling, and ostentation.

THE FIFTH BOOK

I. In the morning when thou findest thyself unwilling to rise, consider with thyself presently, it is to go about a man's work that I am stirred up. Am I then yet unwilling to go about that, for which I myself was born and brought forth into this world? Or was I made for this, to lay me down, and make much of myself in a warm bed? 'O but this is pleasing.' And was it then for this that thou wert born, that thou mightest enjoy pleasure? Was it not in very truth for this, that thou mightest always be busy and in action? Seest thou not how all things in the world besides, how every tree md plant, how sparrows and ants, spiders and bees: how all in their kind are intent as it were orderly to perform whatsoever (towards the preservation of this orderly universe) naturally doth become and belong unto thin? And wilt not thou do that, which belongs unto a man to do? Wilt not thou run to do that, which thy nature doth require? 'But thou must have some rest.' Yes, thou must. Nature hath of that also, as well as of eating and drinking, allowed thee a certain stint. But thou guest beyond thy stint, and beyond that which would suffice, and in matter of action, there thou comest short of that which thou mayest. It must needs be therefore, that thou dost not love thyself, for if thou didst, thou wouldst also love thy nature, and that which thy nature doth propose unto herself as her end. Others, as many as take pleasure in their trade and profession, can even pine themselves at their works, and neglect their bodies and their food for it; and doest thou less honour thy nature, than an ordinary mechanic his trade; or a good dancer his art? than a covetous man his silver, and vainglorious man applause? These to whatsoever they take an affection, can be content to want their meat and sleep, to further that every one which he affects: and shall actions tending to the common good of human society, seem more vile unto thee, or worthy of less respect and intention?

II. How easy a thing is it for a man to put off from him all turbulent adventitious imaginations, and presently to be in perfect rest and tranquillity!

III. Think thyself fit and worthy to speak, or to do anything that is according to nature, and let not the reproach, or report of some that may ensue upon it, ever deter thee. If it be right and honest to be spoken or done, undervalue not thyself so much, as to be discouraged from it. As for them, they have their own rational overruling part, and their own proper inclination: which thou must not stand and look about to take notice of, but go on straight, whither both thine own particular, and the common nature do lead thee; and the way of both these, is but one.

IV. I continue my course by actions according to nature, until I fall and cease, breathing out my last breath into that air, by which continually breathed in I did live; and falling upon that earth, out of whose gifts and fruits my father gathered his seed, my mother her blood, and my nurse her milk, out of which for so many years I have been provided, both of meat and drink. And lastly, which beareth me that tread upon it, and beareth with me that so many ways do abuse it, or so freely make use of it, so many ways to so many ends.

V. No man can admire thee for thy sharp acute language, such is thy natural disability that way. Be it so: yet there be many other good things, for the want of which thou canst not plead the want or natural ability. Let them be seen in thee, which depend wholly from thee; sincerity, gravity, laboriousness, contempt of pleasures; be not querulous, be Content with little, be kind, be free; avoid all superfluity, all vain prattling; be magnanimous. Doest not thou perceive, how many things there be, which notwithstanding any pretence of natural indisposition and unfitness, thou mightest have performed and exhibited, and yet still thou doest voluntarily continue drooping downwards? Or wilt thou say that it is through defect of thy natural constitution, that thou art constrained to murmur, to be base and wretched to flatter; now to accuse, and now to please, and pacify thy body: to be vainglorious, to be so giddy-headed., and unsettled in thy thoughts? nay (witnesses be the Gods) of all these thou mightest have been rid long ago: only, this thou must have been contented with, to have borne the blame of one that is somewhat slow and dull, wherein thou must so exercise thyself, as one who neither doth much take to heart this his natural defect, nor yet pleaseth himself in it.

VI. Such there be, who when they have done a good turn to any, are ready to set them on the score for it, and to require retaliation. Others there be, who though they stand not upon retaliation, to require any, yet they think with themselves nevertheless, that such a one is their debtor, and they know as their word is what they have done. Others again there be, who when they have done any such thing, do not so much as know what they have done; but are like unto the vine, which beareth her grapes, and when once she hath borne her own proper fruit, is contented and seeks for no further recompense. As a horse after a race, and a hunting dog when he hath hunted, and a bee when she hath made her honey, look not for applause and commendation; so neither doth that man that rightly doth understand his own nature when he hath done a good turn: but from one doth proceed to do another, even as the vine after she hath once borne fruit in her own proper season, is ready for another time. Thou therefore must be one of them, who what they do, barely do it without any further thought, and are in a manner insensible of what they do. 'Nay but,' will some reply perchance, 'this very thing a rational man is bound unto, to understand what it is, that he doeth.' For it is the property, say they, of one that is naturally sociable, to be sensible, that he doth operate sociably: nay, and to desire, that the party him self that is sociably dealt with, should be sensible of it too. I answer, That which thou sayest is true indeed, but the true meaning of that which is said, thou dost not understand. And therefore art thou one of those first, whom I mentioned. For they also are led by a probable appearance of reason. But if thou dost desire to understand truly what it is that is said, fear not that thou shalt therefore give over any sociable action.

VII. The form of the Athenians' prayer did run thus: 'O rain, rain, good Jupiter, upon all the grounds and fields that belong to the Athenians.' Either we should not pray at all, or thus absolutely and freely; and not every one for himself in particular alone.

VIII. As we say commonly, The physician hath prescribed unto this man, riding; unto another, cold baths; unto a third, to go barefoot: so it is alike to say, The nature of the universe hath prescribed unto this man sickness, or blindness, or some loss, or damage or some such thing. For as there, when we say of a physician, that he hath prescribed anything, our meaning is, that he hath appointed this for that, as subordinate and conducing to health: so here, whatsoever doth happen unto any, is ordained unto him as a thing subordinate unto the fates, and therefore do we say of such things, that they do συμβαίνειν, that is, happen, or fall together; as of square stones, when either in walls, or pyramids in a certain position they fit one another, and agree as it were in an harmony, the masons say, that they do συμβαίνειν; as if thou shouldest say, fall together: so that in the general, though the things be divers that make it, yet the consent or harmony itself is but one. And as the whole world is made up of all the particular bodies of the world, one perfect and complete body, of the same nature that particular bodies; so is the destiny of particular causes and events one general one, of the same nature that particular causes are. What I now say, even they that are mere idiots are not ignorant of: for they say commonly τοῦτο ἔφερεν ἀυτῷ, that is, This his destiny hath brought upon him. This therefore is by the fates properly and particularly brought upon this, as that unto this in particular is by the physician prescribed. These therefore let us accept of in like manner, as we do those that are prescribed unto us our physicians. For them also in themselves shall We find to contain many harsh things, but we nevertheless, in hope of health, and recovery, accept of them. Let the fulfilling and accomplishment of those things which the common nature hath determined, be unto thee as thy health. Accept then, and be pleased with whatsoever doth happen, though otherwise harsh and un-pleasing, as tending to that end, to the health and welfare of the universe, and to Jove's happiness and prosperity. For this whatsoever it be, should not have been produced, had it not conduced to the good of the universe. For neither doth any ordinary particular nature bring anything to pass, that is not to whatsoever is within the sphere of its own proper administration and government agreeable and subordinate. For these two considerations then thou must be well pleased with anything that doth happen unto thee. First, because that for thee properly it was brought to pass, and unto thee it was prescribed; and that from the very beginning by the series and connection of the first causes, it hath ever had a reference unto thee. And secondly, because the good success and perfect welfare, and indeed the very continuance of Him, that is the Administrator of the whole, doth in a manner depend on it. For the whole (because whole, therefore entire and perfect) is maimed, and mutilated, if thou shalt cut off anything at all, whereby the coherence, and contiguity as of parts, so of causes, is maintained and preserved. Of which certain it is, that thou doest (as much as lieth in thee) cut off, and in some sort violently take somewhat away, as often as thou art displeased with anything that happeneth.

IX. Be not discontented, be not disheartened, be not out of hope, if often it succeed not so well with thee punctually and precisely to do all things according to the right dogmata, but being once cast off, return unto them again: and as for those many and more frequent occurrences, either of worldly distractions, or human infirmities, which as a man thou canst not but in some measure be subject unto, be not thou discontented with them; but however, love and affect that only which thou dust return unto: a philosopher's life, and proper occupation after the most exact manner. And when thou dust return to thy philosophy, return not unto it as the manner of some is, after play and liberty as it were, to their schoolmasters and pedagogues; but as they that have sore eyes to their sponge and egg: or as another to his cataplasm; or as others to their fomentations: so shalt not thou make it a matter of ostentation at all to obey reason but of ease and comfort. And remember that philosophy requireth nothing of thee, but what thy nature requireth, and wouldest thou thyself desire anything that is not according to nature? for which of these sayest thou; that which is according to nature or against it, is of itself more kind and pleasing? Is it not for that respect especially, that pleasure itself is to so many men's hurt and overthrow, most prevalent, because esteemed commonly most kind, and natural? But consider well whether magnanimity rather, and true liberty, and true simplicity, and equanimity, and holiness; whether these be not most kind and natural? And prudency itself, what more kind and amiable than it, when thou shalt truly consider with thyself, what it is through all the proper objects of thy rational intellectual faculty currently to go on without any fall or stumble? As for the things of the world, their true nature is in a manner so involved with obscurity, that unto many philosophers, and those no mean ones, they seemed altogether incomprehensible, and the Stoics themselves, though they judge them not altogether incomprehensible, yet scarce and not without much difficulty, comprehensible, so that all assent of ours is fallible, for who is he that is infallible in his conclusions? From the nature of things, pass now unto their subjects and matter: how temporary, how vile are they I such as may be in the power and possession of some abominable loose liver, of some common strumpet, of some notorious oppressor and extortioner. Pass from thence to the dispositions of them that thou doest ordinarily converse with, how hardly do we bear, even with the most loving and amiable! that I may not say, how hard it is for us to bear even with our own selves, in such obscurity, and impurity of things: in such and so continual a flux both of the substances and time; both of the motions themselves, and things moved; what it is that we can fasten upon; either to honour, and respect especially; or seriously, and studiously to seek after; I cannot so much as conceive For indeed they are things contrary.

X. Thou must comfort thyself in the expectation of thy natural dissolution, and in the meantime not grieve at the delay; but rest contented in those two things. First, that nothing shall happen unto thee, which is not according to the nature of the universe. Secondly, that it is in thy power, to do nothing against thine own proper God, and inward spirit. For it is not in any man's power to constrain thee to transgress against him.

XI. What is the use that now at this present I make of my soul? Thus from time to time and upon all occasions thou must put this question to thyself; what is now that part of mine which they call the rational mistress part, employed about? Whose soul do I now properly possess? a child's? or a youth's? a woman's? or a tyrant's? some brute, or some wild beast's soul?

XII. What those things are in themselves, which by the greatest part are esteemed good, thou mayest gather even from this. For if a man shall hear things mentioned as good, which are really good indeed, such as are prudence, temperance, justice, fortitude, after so much heard and conceived, he cannot endure to hear of any more, for the word good is properly spoken of them. But as for those which by the vulgar are esteemed good, if he shall hear them mentioned as good, he doth hearken for more. He is well contented to hear, that what is spoken by the comedian, is but familiarly and popularly spoken, so that even the vulgar apprehend the difference. For why is it else, that this offends not and needs not to be excused, when virtues are styled good: but that which is spoken in commendation of wealth, pleasure, or honour, we entertain it only as merrily and pleasantly spoken? Proceed therefore, and inquire further, whether it may not be that those things also which being mentioned upon the stage were merrily, and with great applause of the multitude, scoffed at with this jest, that they that possessed them had not in all the world of their own, (such was their affluence and plenty) so much as a place where to avoid their excrements. Whether, I say, those ought not also in very deed to be much respected, and esteemed of, as the only things that are truly good.

XIII. All that I consist of, is either form or matter. No corruption can reduce either of these unto nothing: for neither did I of nothing become a subsistent creature. Every part of mine then will by mutation be disposed into a certain part of the whole world, and that in time into another part; and so *in infinitum;* by which kind of mutation, I also became what I am, and so did they that begot me, and they before them, and so upwards *in infinitum*. For so we may be allowed to speak, though the age and government of the world, be to some certain periods of time limited, and confined.

XIV. Reason, and rational power, are faculties which content themselves with themselves, and their own proper operations. And as for their first inclination and motion, that they take from themselves. But their progress is right to the end and object, which is in their way, as it were, and lieth just before them: that is, which is feasible and possible, whether it be that which at the first they proposed to themselves, or no. For which reason also such actions are termed κατορθώσεις, to intimate the directness of the way, by which they are achieved. Nothing must be thought to belong to a man, which doth not belong unto him as he is a man. These, the event of purposes, are not things required in a man. The nature of man doth not profess any such things. The final ends and consummations of actions are nothing at all to a man's nature. The end therefore of a man, or the *summum bonum* whereby that end is fulfilled, cannot consist in the consummation of actions purposed and intended. Again, concerning these outward worldly things, were it so that any of them did properly belong unto man, then would it not belong unto man, to condemn them and to stand in opposition with them. Neither would he be praiseworthy that can live without them; or he good, (if these were good indeed) who of his own accord doth deprive himself of any of them. But we see contrariwise, that the more a man doth withdraw himself from these wherein external pomp and greatness doth consist, or any other like these; or the better he doth bear with the loss of these, the better he is accounted.

XV. Such as thy thoughts and ordinary cogitations are, such will thy mind be in time. For the soul doth as it were receive its tincture from the fancies, and imaginations. Dye it therefore and thoroughly soak it with the assiduity of these cogitations. As for example. Wheresoever thou mayest live, there it is in thy power to live well and happy. But thou mayest live at the Court, there then also mayest thou live well and happy. Again, that which everything is made for, he is also made unto that, and cannot but naturally incline unto it. That which anything doth naturally incline unto, therein is his end.

Wherein the end of everything doth consist, therein also doth his good and benefit consist. Society therefore is the proper good of a rational creature. For that we are made for society, it hath long since been demonstrated. Or can any man make any question of this, that whatsoever is naturally worse and inferior, is ordinarily subordinated to that which is better? and that those things that are best, are made one for another? And those things that have souls, are better than those that have none? and of those that have, those best that have rational souls?

XVI. To desire things impossible is the part of a mad man. But it is a thing impossible, that wicked man should not commit some such things. Neither doth anything happen to any man, which in the ordinary course of nature as natural unto him doth not happen. Again, the same things happen unto others also. And truly, if either he that is ignorant that such a thing hath happened unto him, or he that is ambitious to be commended for his magnanimity, can be patient, and is not grieved: is it not a grievous thing, that either ignorance, or a vain desire to please and to be commended, should be more powerful and effectual than true prudence? As for the things themselves, they touch not the soul, neither can they have any access unto it: neither can they of themselves any ways either affect it, or move it. For she herself alone can affect and move herself, and according as the dogmata and opinions are, which she doth vouchsafe herself; so are those things which, as accessories, have any co-existence with her.

XVII. After one consideration, man is nearest unto us; as we are bound to do them good, and to bear with them. But as he may oppose any of our true proper actions, so man is unto me but as a thing indifferent: even as the sun, or the wind, or some wild beast. By some of these it may be, that some operation or other of mine, may be hindered; however, of my mind and resolution itself, there can be no let or impediment, by reason of that ordinary constant both exception (or reservation wherewith it inclineth) and ready conversion of objects; from that which may not be, to that which may be, which in the prosecution of its inclinations, as occasion serves, it doth observe. For by these the mind doth turn and convert any impediment whatsoever, to be her aim and purpose. So that what before was the impediment, is now the principal object of her working; and that which before was in her way, is now her readiest way.

XVIII. Honour that which is chiefest and most powerful in the world, and that is it, which makes use of all things, and governs all things. So also in thyself; honour that which is chiefest, and most powerful; and is of one kind and nature with that which we now spake of. For it is the very same, which being in thee, turneth all other things to its own use, and by whom also thy life is governed.

XIX. That which doth not hurt the city itself; cannot hurt any citizen. This rule thou must remember to apply and make use of upon every conceit and apprehension of wrong. If the whole city be not hurt by this, neither am I certainly. And if the whole be not, why should I make it my private grievance? consider rather what it is wherein he is overseen that is thought to have done the wrong. Again, often meditate how swiftly all things that subsist, and all things that are done in the world, are carried away, and as it were conveyed out of sight: for both the substance themselves, we see as a flood, are in a continual flux; and all actions in a perpetual change; and the causes themselves, subject to a thousand alterations, neither is there anything almost, that may ever be said to be now settled and constant. Next unto this, and which follows upon it, consider both the infiniteness of the time already past, and the immense vastness of that which is to come, wherein all things are to be resolved and annihilated. Art not thou then a very fool, who for these things, art either puffed up with pride, or distracted with cares, or canst find in thy heart to make such moans as for a thing that would trouble thee for a very long time? Consider the whole universe whereof thou art but a very little part, and the whole age of the world together, whereof but a short and very momentary portion is allotted unto thee, and all the fates and destinies together, of which how much is it that comes to thy part and share! Again: another doth trespass against me. Let him look to that. He is master of his own disposition, and of his own operation. I for my part am in the meantime in possession of as much, as the common nature would have me to possess: and that which mine own nature would have me do, I do.

XX. Let not that chief commanding part of thy soul be ever subject to any variation through any corporal either pain or pleasure, neither suffer it to be mixed with these, but let it both circumscribe itself, and confine those affections to their own proper parts and members. But if at any time they do reflect and rebound upon the mind and understanding (as in an united and compacted body it must needs;) then must thou not go about to resist sense and feeling, it being natural. However let not thy understanding to this natural sense and feeling, which whether unto our flesh pleasant or painful, is unto us nothing properly, add an opinion of either good or bad and all is well.

XXI. To live with the Gods. He liveth with the Gods, who at all times affords unto them the spectacle of a soul, both contented and well pleased with whatsoever is afforded, or allotted unto her; and performing whatsoever is pleasing to that Spirit, whom (being part of himself) Jove hath appointed to every man as his overseer and governor.

XXII. Be not angry neither with him whose breath, neither with him whose arm holes, are offensive. What can he do? such is his breath naturally, and such are his arm holes; and from such, such an effect, and such a smell must of necessity proceed. 'O, but the man (sayest thou) hath understanding in him, and might of himself know, that he by standing near, cannot choose but offend.' And thou also (God bless thee!) hast understanding. Let thy reasonable faculty, work upon his reasonable faculty; show him his fault, admonish him. If he hearken unto thee, thou hast cured him, and there will be no more occasion of anger.

XXIII. 'Where there shall neither roarer be, nor harlot.' Why so? As thou dost purpose to live, when thou hast retired thyself to some such place, where neither roarer nor harlot is: so mayest thou here. And if they will not suffer thee, then mayest thou leave thy life rather than thy calling, but so as one that doth not think himself anyways wronged. Only as one would say, Here is a smoke; I will out of it. And what a great matter is this! Now till some such thing force me out, I will continue free; neither shall any man hinder me to do what I will, and my will shall ever be by the proper nature of a reasonable and sociable creature, regulated and directed.

XXIV. That rational essence by which the universe is governed, is for community and society; and therefore hath it both made the things that are worse, for the best, and hath allied and knit together those which are best, as it were in an harmony. Seest thou not how it hath subordinated, and co-ordinated? and how it hath distributed unto everything according to its worth? and those which have the pre-eminency and superiority above all, hath it united together, into a mutual consent and agreement.

XXV. How hast thou carried thyself hitherto towards the Gods? towards thy parents? towards thy brethren? towards thy wife? towards thy children? towards thy masters? thy foster-fathers? thy friends? thy domestics? thy servants? Is it so with thee, that hitherto thou hast neither by word or deed wronged any of them? Remember withal through how many things thou hast already passed, and how many thou hast been able to endure; so that now the legend of thy life is full, and thy charge is accomplished. Again, how many truly good things have certainly by thee been discerned? how many pleasures, how many pains hast thou passed over with contempt? how many things eternally glorious hast thou despised? towards how many perverse unreasonable men hast thou carried thyself kindly, and discreetly?

XXVI. Why should imprudent unlearned souls trouble that which is both learned, and prudent? And which is that that is so? she that understandeth the beginning and the end, and hath the true knowledge of that rational essence, that passeth through all things subsisting, and through all ages being ever the same, disposing and dispensing as it were this universe by certain periods of time.

XXVII. Within a very little while, thou wilt be either ashes, or a sceletum; and a name perchance; and perchance, not so much as a name. And what is that but an empty sound, and a rebounding echo? Those things which in this life are dearest unto us, and of most account, they are in themselves but vain, putrid, contemptible. The most weighty and serious, if rightly esteemed, but as puppies, biting one another: or untoward children, now laughing and then crying. As for faith, and modesty, and justice, and truth, they long since, as one of the poets hath it, have abandoned this spacious earth, and retired themselves unto heaven. What is it then that doth keep thee here, if things sensible be so mutable and unsettled? and the senses so obscure, and so fallible? and our souls nothing but an exhalation of blood? and to be in credit among such, be but vanity? What is it that thou dost stay for? an extinction, or a translation; either of them with a propitious and contented mind. But still that time come, what will content thee? what else, but to worship and praise the Gods; and to do good unto men. To bear with them, and to forbear to do them any wrong. And for all external things belonging either to this thy wretched body, or life, to remember that they are neither thine, nor in thy power.

XXVIII. Thou mayest always speed, if thou wilt but make choice of the right way; if in the course both of thine opinions and actions, thou wilt observe a true method. These two things be common to the souls, as of God, so of men, and of every reasonable creature, first that in their own proper work they cannot be hindered by anything: and secondly, that their happiness doth consist in a disposition to, and in the practice of righteousness; and that in these their desire is terminated.

XXIX. If this neither be my wicked act, nor an act anyways depending from any wickedness of mine, and that by it the public is not hurt; what doth it concern me? And wherein can the public be hurt? For thou must not altogether be carried by conceit and common opinion: as for help thou must afford that unto them after thy best ability, and as occasion shall require, though they sustain damage, but in these middle or worldly things; but however do not thou conceive that they are truly hurt thereby: for that is not right. But as that old foster-father in the comedy, being now to take his leave doth with a great deal of ceremony, require his foster-child's rhombus, or rattle-top, remembering nevertheless that it is but a rhombus; so here also do thou likewise. For indeed what is all this pleading and public bawling for at the courts? O man, hast thou forgotten what those things are! yea but they are things that others much care for, and highly esteem of. Wilt thou therefore be a fool too? Once I was; let that suffice.

XXX. Let death surprise me when it will, and where it will, I may be εὔμοιρος, or a happy man, nevertheless.

For he is a happy man, who in his lifetime dealeth unto himself a happy lot and portion. A happy lot and portion is, good inclinations of the soul, good desires, good actions.

THE SIXTH BOOK

I. The matter itself, of which the universe doth consist, is of itself very tractable and pliable. That rational essence that doth govern it, hath in itself no cause to do evil. It hath no evil in itself; neither can it do anything that is evil: neither can anything be hurt by it. And all things are done and determined according to its will and prescript.

II. Be it all one unto thee, whether half frozen or well warm; whether only slumbering, or after a full sleep; whether discommended or commended thou do thy duty: or whether dying or doing somewhat else; for that also 'to die,' must among the rest be reckoned as one of the duties and actions of our lives.

III. Look in, let not either the proper quality, or the true worth of anything pass thee, before thou hast fully apprehended it.

IV. All substances come soon to their change, and either they shall be resolved by way of exhalation (if so be that all things shall be reunited into one substance), or as others maintain, they shall be scattered and dispersed. As for that Rational Essence by which all things are governed, as it best understandeth itself, both its own disposition, and what it doth, and what matter it hath to do with and accordingly doth all things; so we that do not, no wonder, if we wonder at many things, the reasons whereof we cannot comprehend.

V. The best kind of revenge is, not to become like unto them. VI. Let this be thy only joy, and thy only comfort, from one sociable kind action without intermission to pass unto another, God being ever in thy mind.

VII. The rational commanding part, as it alone can stir up and turn itself; so it maketh both itself to be, and everything that happeneth, to appear unto itself, as it will itself.

VIII. According to the nature of the universe all things particular are determined, not according to any other nature, either about compassing and containing; or within, dispersed and contained; or without, depending. Either this universe is a mere confused mass, and an intricate context of things, which shall in time be scattered and dispersed again: or it is an union consisting of order, and administered by Providence. If the first, why should I desire to continue any longer in this fortuit confusion and commixtion? or why should I take care for anything else, but that as soon as may be I may be earth again? And why should I trouble myself any more whilst I seek to please the Gods? Whatsoever I do, dispersion is my end, and will come upon me whether I will or no. But if the latter be, then am not I religious in vain; then will I be quiet and patient, and put my trust in Him, who is the Governor of all.

IX. Whensoever by some present hard occurrences thou art constrained to be in some sort troubled and vexed, return unto thyself as soon as may be, and be not out of tune longer than thou must needs. For so shalt thou be the better able to keep thy part another time, and to maintain the harmony, if thou dost use thyself to this continually; once out, presently to have recourse unto it, and to begin again.

X. If it were that thou hadst at one time both a stepmother, and a natural mother living, thou wouldst honour and respect her also; nevertheless to thine own natural mother would thy refuge, and recourse be continually. So let the court and thy philosophy be unto thee. Have recourse unto it often, and comfort thyself in her, by whom it is that those other things are made tolerable unto thee, and thou also in those things not intolerable unto others.

XI. How marvellous useful it is for a man to represent unto himself meats, and all such things that are for the mouth, under a right apprehension and imagination! as for example: This is the carcass of a fish; this of a bird; and this of a hog. And again more generally; This phalernum, this excellent highly commended wine, is but the bare juice of an ordinary grape. This purple robe, but sheep's hairs, dyed with the blood of a shellfish. So for coitus, it is but the attrition of an ordinary base entrail, and the excretion of a little vile snivel, with a certain kind of convulsion: according to Hippocrates his opinion. How excellent useful are these lively fancies and representations of things, thus penetrating and passing through the objects, to make their true nature known and apparent! This must thou use all thy life long, and upon all occasions: and then especially, when matters are apprehended as of great worth and respect, thy art and care must be to uncover them, and to behold their vileness, and to take away from them all those serious circumstances and expressions, under which they made so grave a show. For outward pomp and appearance is a great juggler; and then especially art thou most in danger to be beguiled by it, when (to a man's thinking) thou most seemest to be employed about matters of moment.

XII. See what Crates pronounceth concerning Xenocrates himself. XIII. Those things which the common sort of people do admire, are most of them such things as are very general, and may be comprehended under things merely natural, or naturally affected and qualified: as stones, wood, figs, vines, olives. Those that be admired by them that are more moderate and restrained, are comprehended under things animated: as flocks and herds. Those that are yet more gentle and curious, their admiration is commonly confined to reasonable creatures only; not in general as they are reasonable, but as they are capable of art, or of some craft and subtile invention: or perchance barely to reasonable creatures; as they that delight in the possession of many slaves. But he that honours a reasonable soul in general, as it is reasonable and naturally sociable, doth little regard anything else: and above all things is careful to preserve his own, in the continual habit and exercise both of reason and sociableness: and thereby doth co-operate with him, of whose nature he doth also participate; God.

XIV. Some things hasten to be, and others to be no more. And even whatsoever now is, some part thereof hath already perished. Perpetual fluxes and alterations renew the world, as the perpetual course of time doth make the age of the world (of itself infinite) to appear always fresh and new. In such a flux and course of all things, what of these things that hasten so fast away should any man regard, since among all there is not any that a man may fasten and fix upon? as if a man would settle his affection upon some ordinary sparrow living by him, who is no sooner seen, than out of sight. For we must not think otherwise of our lives, than as a mere exhalation of blood, or of an ordinary respiration of air. For what in our common apprehension is, to breathe in the air and to breathe it out again, which we do daily: so much is it and no more, at once to breathe out all thy respirative faculty into that common air from whence but lately (as being but from yesterday, and to-day), thou didst first breathe it in, and with it, life.

XV. Not vegetative spiration, it is not surely (which plants have) that in this life should be so dear unto us; nor sensitive respiration, the proper life of beasts, both tame and wild; nor this our imaginative faculty; nor that we are subject to be led and carried up and down by the strength of our sensual appetites; or that we can gather, and live together; or that we can feed: for that in effect is no better, than that we can void the excrements of our food. What is it then that should be dear unto us? to hear a clattering noise? if not that, then neither to be applauded by the tongues of men. For the praises of many tongues, is in effect no better than the clattering of so many tongues. If then neither applause, what is there remaining that should be dear unto thee? This I think: that in all thy motions and actions thou be moved, and restrained according to thine own true natural constitution and Construction only. And to this even ordinary arts and professions do lead us. For it is that which every art doth aim at, that whatsoever it is, that is by art effected and prepared, may be fit for that work that it is prepared for. This is the end that he that dresseth the vine, and he that takes upon him either to tame colts, or to train up dogs, doth aim at. What else doth the education of children, and all learned professions tend unto? Certainly then it is that, which should be dear unto us also. If in this particular it go well with thee, care not for the obtaining of other things. But is it so, that thou canst not but respect other things also? Then canst not thou truly be free? then canst thou not have self-content: then wilt thou ever be subject to passions. For it is not possible, but that thou must be envious, and jealous, and suspicious of them whom thou knowest can bereave thee of such things; and again, a secret underminer of them, whom thou seest in present possession of that which is dear unto thee. To be short, he must of necessity be full of confusion within himself, and often accuse the Gods, whosoever stands in need of these things. But if thou shalt honour and respect thy mind only, that will make thee acceptable towards thyself, towards thy friends very tractable; and conformable and concordant with the Gods; that is, accepting with praises whatsoever they shall think good to appoint and allot unto thee.

XVI. Under, above, and about, are the motions of the elements; but the motion of virtue, is none of those motions, but is somewhat more excellent and divine. Whose way (to speed and prosper in it) must be through a way, that is not easily comprehended.

XVII. Who can choose but wonder at them? They will not speak well of them that are at the same time with them, and live with them; yet they themselves are very ambitious, that they that shall follow, whom they have never seen, nor shall ever see, should speak well of them. As if a man should grieve that he hath not been commended by them, that lived before him.

XVIII. Do not ever conceive anything impossible to man, which by thee cannot, or not without much difficulty be effected; but whatsoever in general thou canst Conceive possible and proper unto any man, think that very possible unto thee also.

XIX. Suppose that at the palestra somebody hath all to-torn thee with his nails, and hath broken thy head. Well, thou art wounded. Yet thou dost not exclaim; thou art not offended with him. Thou dost not suspect him for it afterwards, as one that watcheth to do thee a mischief. Yea even then, though thou dost thy best to save thyself from him, yet not from him as an enemy. It is not by way of any suspicious indignation, but by way of gentle and friendly declination. Keep the same mind and disposition in other parts of thy life also. For many things there be, which we must conceit and apprehend, as though we had had to do with an antagonist at the palestra. For as I said, it is very possible for us to avoid and decline, though we neither suspect, nor hate.

XX. If anybody shall reprove me, and shall make it apparent unto me, that in any either opinion or action of mine I do err, I will most gladly retract. For it is the truth that I seek after, by which I am sure that never any man was hurt; and as sure, that he is hurt that continueth in any error, or ignorance whatsoever.

XXI. I for my part will do what belongs unto me; as for other things, whether things unsensible or things irrational; or if rational, yet deceived and ignorant of the true way, they shall not trouble or distract me. For as for those creatures which are not endued with reason and all other things and-matters of the world whatsoever I freely, and generously, as one endued with reason, of things that have none, make use of them. And as for men, towards them as naturally partakers of the same reason, my care is to carry myself sociably. But whatsoever it is that thou art about, remember to call upon the Gods. And as for the time how long thou shalt live to do these things, let it be altogether indifferent unto thee, for even three such hours are sufficient.

XXII. Alexander of Macedon, and he that dressed his mules, when once dead both came to one. For either they were both resumed into those original rational essences from whence all things in the world are propagated; or both after one fashion were scattered into atoms.

XXIII Consider how many different things, whether they concern our bodies, or our souls, in a moment of time come to pass in every one of us, and so thou wilt not wonder if many more things or rather all things that are done, can at one time subsist, and coexist in that both one and general, which we call the world.

XXIV. if any should put this question unto thee, how this word Antoninus is written, wouldst thou not presently fix thine intention upon it, and utter out in order every letter of it? And if any shall begin to gainsay thee, and quarrel with thee about it; wilt thou quarrel with him again, or rather go on meekly as thou hast begun, until thou hast numbered out every letter? Here then likewise remember, that every duty that belongs unto a man doth consist of some certain letters or numbers as it were, to which without any noise or tumult keeping thyself thou must orderly proceed to thy proposed end, forbearing to quarrel with him that would quarrel and fall out with thee.

XXV. Is it not a cruel thing to forbid men to affect those things, which they conceive to agree best with their own natures, and to tend most to their own proper good and behoof? But thou after a sort deniest them this liberty, as often as thou art angry with them for their sins. For surely they are led unto those sins whatsoever they be, as to their proper good and commodity. But it is not so (thou wilt object perchance). Thou therefore teach them better, and make it appear unto them: but be not thou angry with them.

XXVI. Death is a cessation from the impression of the senses, the tyranny of the passions, the errors of the mind, and the servitude of the body.

XXVII. If in this kind of life thy body be able to hold out, it is a shame that thy soul should faint first, and give over, take heed, lest of a philosopher thou become a mere Cæsar in time, and receive a new tincture from the court. For it may happen if thou dost not take heed. Keep thyself therefore, truly simple, good, sincere, grave, free from all ostentation, a lover of that which is just, religious, kind, tender-hearted, strong and vigorous to undergo anything that becomes thee. Endeavour to continue such, as philosophy (hadst thou wholly and constantly applied thyself unto it) would have made, and secured thee. Worship the Gods, procure the welfare of men, this life is short. Charitable actions, and a holy disposition, is the only fruit of this earthly life.

XXVIII. Do all things as becometh the disciple of Antoninus Pius. Remember his resolute constancy in things that were done by him according to reason, his equability in all things, his sanctity; the cheerfulness of his countenance, his sweetness, and how free he was from all vainglory; how careful to come to the true and exact knowledge of matters in hand, and how he would by no means give over till he did fully, and plainly understand the whole state of the business; and how patiently, and without any contestation he would bear with them, that did unjustly condemn him: how he would never be over-hasty in anything, nor give ear to slanders and false accusations, but examine and observe with best diligence the several actions and dispositions of men. Again, how he was no backbiter, nor easily frightened, nor suspicious, and in his language free from all affectation and curiosity: and how easily he would content himself with few things, as lodging, bedding, clothing, and ordinary nourishment, and attendance. How able to endure labour, how patient; able through his spare diet to continue from morning to evening without any necessity of withdrawing before his accustomed hours to the necessities of nature: his uniformity and constancy in matter of friendship. How he would bear with them that with all boldness and liberty opposed his opinions; and even rejoice if any man could better advise him: and lastly, how religious he was without superstition. All these things of him remember, that whensoever thy last hour shall come upon thee, it may find thee, as it did him, ready for it in the possession of a good conscience.

XXIX. Stir up thy mind, and recall thy wits again from thy natural dreams, and visions, and when thou art perfectly awoken, and canst perceive that they were but dreams that troubled thee, as one newly awakened out of another kind of sleep look upon these worldly things with the same mind as thou didst upon those, that thou sawest in thy sleep.

XXX. I consist of body and soul. Unto my body all things are indifferent, for of itself it cannot affect one thing more than another with apprehension of any difference; as for my mind, all things which are not within the verge of her own operation, are indifferent unto her, and for her own operations, those altogether depend of her; neither does she busy herself about any, but those that are present; for as for future and past operations, those also are now at this present indifferent unto her.

XXXI. As long as the foot doth that which belongeth unto it to do, and the hand that which belongs unto it, their labour, whatsoever it be, is not unnatural. So a man as long as he doth that which is proper unto a man, his labour cannot be against nature; and if it be not against nature, then neither is it hurtful unto him. But if it were so that happiness did consist in pleasure: how came notorious robbers, impure abominable livers, parricides, and tyrants, in so large a measure to have their part of pleasures?

XXXII. Dost thou not see, how even those that profess mechanic arts, though in some respect they be no better than mere idiots, yet they stick close to the course of their trade, neither can they find in their heart to decline from it: and is it not a grievous thing that an architect, or a physician shall respect the course and mysteries of their profession, more than a man the proper course and condition of his own nature, reason, which is common to him and to the Gods?

XXXIII. Asia, Europe; what are they, but as corners of the whole world; of which the whole sea, is but as one drop; and the great Mount Athos, but as a clod, as all present time is but as one point of eternity. All, petty things; all things that are soon altered, soon perished. And all things come from one beginning; either all severally and particularly deliberated and resolved upon, by the general ruler and governor of all; or all by necessary consequence. So that the dreadful hiatus of a gaping lion, and all poison, and all hurtful things, are but (as the thorn and the mire) the necessary consequences of goodly fair things. Think not of these therefore, as things contrary to those which thou dost much honour, and respect; but consider in thy mind the true fountain of all.

XXXIV He that seeth the things that are now, hath Seen all that either was ever, or ever shall be, for all things are of one kind; and all like one unto another. Meditate often upon the connection of all things in the world; and upon the mutual relation that they have one unto another. For all things are after a sort folded and involved one within another, and by these means all agree well together. For one thing is consequent unto another, by local motion, by natural conspiration and agreement, and by substantial union, or, reduction of all substances into one.

XXXV. Fit and accommodate thyself to that estate and to those occurrences, which by the destinies have been annexed unto thee; and love those men whom thy fate it is to live with; but love them truly. An instrument, a tool, an utensil, whatsoever it be, if it be fit for the purpose it was made for, it is as it should be though he perchance that made and fitted it, be out of sight and gone. But in things natural, that power which hath framed and fitted them, is and abideth within them still: for which reason she ought also the more to be respected, and we are the more obliged (if we may live and pass our time according to her purpose and intention) to think that all is well with us, and according to our own minds. After this manner also, and in this respect it is, that he that is all in all doth enjoy his happiness.

XXXVI. What things soever are not within the proper power and jurisdiction of thine own will either to compass or avoid, if thou shalt propose unto thyself any of those things as either good, or evil; it must needs be that according as thou shalt either fall into that which thou dost think evil, or miss of that which thou dost think good, so wilt thou be ready both to complain of the Gods, and to hate those men, who either shall be so indeed, or shall by thee be suspected as the cause either of thy missing of the one, or falling into the other. And indeed we must needs commit many evils, if we incline to any of these things, more or less, with an opinion of any difference. But if we mind and fancy those things only, as good and bad, which wholly depend of our own wills, there is no more occasion why we should either murmur against the Gods, or be at enmity with any man.

XXXVII. We all work to one effect, some willingly, and with a rational apprehension of what we do: others without any such knowledge. As I think Heraclitus in a place speaketh of them that sleep, that even they do work in their kind, and do confer to the general operations of the world. One man therefore doth co-operate after one sort, and another after another sort; but even he that doth murmur, and to his power doth resist and hinder; even he as much as any doth co-operate. For of such also did the world stand in need. Now do thou consider among which of these thou wilt rank thyself. For as for him who is the Administrator of all, he will make good use of thee whether thou wilt or no, and make thee (as a part and member of the whole) so to co-operate with him, that whatsoever thou doest, shall turn to the furtherance of his own counsels, and resolutions. But be not thou for shame such a part of the whole, as that vile and ridiculous verse (which Chrysippus in a place doth mention) is a part of the comedy.

XXXVIII. Doth either the sun take upon him to do that which belongs to the rain? or his son Aesculapius that, which unto the earth doth properly belong? How is it with every one of the stars in particular? Though they all differ one from another, and have their several charges and functions by themselves, do they not all nevertheless concur and co- operate to one end?

XXXIX. If so be that the Gods have deliberated in particular of those things that should happen unto me, I must stand to their deliberation, as discrete and wise. For that a God should be an imprudent God, is a thing hard even to conceive: and why should they resolve to do me hurt? for what profit either unto them or the universe (which they specially take care for) could arise from it? But if so be that they have not deliberated of me in particular, certainly they have of the whole in general, and those things which in consequence and coherence of this general deliberation happen unto me in particular, I am bound to embrace and accept of. But if so be that they have not deliberated at all (which indeed is very irreligious for any man to believe: for then let us neither sacrifice, nor pray, nor respect our oaths, neither let us any more use any of those things, which we persuaded of the presence and secret conversation of the Gods among us, daily use and practise:) but, I say, if so be that they have not indeed either in general, or particular deliberated of any of those things, that happen unto us in this world; yet God be thanked, that of those things that concern myself, it is lawful for me to deliberate myself, and all my deliberation is but concerning that which may be to me most profitable. Now that unto every one is most profitable, which is according to his own constitution and nature. And my nature is, to be rational in all my actions and as a good, and natural member of a city and commonwealth, towards my fellow members ever to be sociably and kindly disposed and affected. My city and country as I am Antoninus, is Rome; as a man, the whole world. Those things therefore that are expedient and profitable to those cities, are the only things that are good and expedient for me.

XL. Whatsoever in any kind doth happen to any one, is expedient to the whole. And thus much to content us might suffice, that it is expedient for the whole in general. But yet this also shalt thou generally perceive, if thou dost diligently take heed, that whatsoever doth happen to any one man or men.... And now I am content that the word expedient, should more generally be understood of those things which we otherwise call middle things, or things indifferent; as health, wealth, and the like.

XLI. As the ordinary shows of the theatre and of other such places, when thou art presented with them, affect thee; as the same things still seen, and in the same fashion, make the sight ingrateful and tedious; so must all the things that we see all our life long affect us. For all things, above and below, are still the same, and from the same causes. When then will there be an end?

XLII. Let the several deaths of men of all sorts, and of all sorts of professions, and of all sort of nations, be a perpetual object of thy thoughts,... so that thou mayst even come down to Philistio, Phœbus, and Origanion. Pass now to other generations. Thither shall we after many changes, where so many brave orators are; where so many grave philosophers; Heraclitus, Pythagoras,

Socrates. Where so many heroes of the old times; and then so many brave captains of the latter times; and so many kings. After all these, where Eudoxus, Hipparchus, Archimedes; where so many other sharp, generous, industrious, subtile, peremptory dispositions; and among others, even they, that have been the greatest scoffers and deriders of the frailty and brevity of this our human life; as Menippus, and others, as many as there have been such as he. Of all these consider, that they long since are all dead, and gone. And what do they suffer by it! Nay they that have not so much as a name remaining, what are they the worse for it? One thing there is, and that only, which is worth our while in this world, and ought by us much to be esteemed; and that is, according to truth and righteousness, meekly and lovingly to converse with false, and unrighteous men.

XLIII. When thou wilt comfort and cheer thyself, call to mind the several gifts and virtues of them, whom thou dost daily converse with; as for example, the industry of the one; the modesty of another; the liberality of a third; of another some other thing. For nothing can so much rejoice thee, as the resemblances and parallels of several virtues, visible and eminent in the dispositions of those who live with thee; especially when, all at once, as near as may be, they represent themselves unto thee. And therefore thou must have them always in a readiness.

XLIV. Dost thou grieve that thou dost weigh but so many pounds, and not three hundred rather? Just as much reason hast thou to grieve that thou must live but so many years, and not longer. For as for bulk and substance thou dost content thyself with that proportion of it that is allotted unto thee, so shouldst thou for time.

XLV. Let us do our best endeavours to persuade them; but however, if reason and justice lead thee to it, do it, though they be never so much against it. But if any shall by force withstand thee, and hinder thee in it, convert thy virtuous inclination from one object unto another, from justice to contented equanimity, and cheerful patience: so that what in the one is thy hindrance, thou mayst make use of it for the exercise of another virtue: and remember that it was with due exception, and reservation, that thou didst at first incline and desire. For thou didst not set thy mind upon things impossible. Upon what then? that all thy desires might ever be moderated with this due kind of reservation. And this thou hast, and mayst always obtain, whether the thing desired be in thy power or no. And what do I care for more, if that for which I was born and brought forth into the world (to rule all my desires with reason and discretion) may be?

XLVI. The ambitious supposeth another man's act, praise and applause, to be his own happiness; the voluptuous his own sense and feeling; but he that is wise, his own action.

XLVII. It is in thy power absolutely to exclude all manner of conceit and opinion, as concerning this matter; and by the same means, to exclude all grief and sorrow from thy soul. For as for the things and objects themselves, they of themselves have no such power, whereby to beget and force upon us any opinion at all.

XLVIII. Use thyself when any man speaks unto thee, so to hearken unto him, as that in the interim thou give not way to any other thoughts; that so thou mayst (as far as is possible) seem fixed and fastened to his very soul, whosoever he be that speaks unto thee.

XLIX. That which is not good for the bee-hive, cannot be good for the bee.

L. Will either passengers, or patients, find fault and complain, either the one if they be well carried, or the others if well cured? Do they take care for any more than this; the one, that their shipmaster may bring them safe to land, and the other, that their physician may effect their recovery?

LI. How many of them who came into the world at the same time when I did, are already gone out of it?

LII. To them that are sick of the jaundice, honey seems bitter; and to them that are bitten by a mad dog, the water terrible; and to children, a little ball seems a fine thing. And why then should I be angry? or do I think that error and false opinion is less powerful to make men transgress, than either choler, being immoderate and excessive, to cause the jaundice; or poison, to cause rage?

LIII. No man can hinder thee to live as thy nature doth require. Nothing can happen unto thee, but what the common good of nature doth require.

LIV. What manner of men they be whom they seek to please, and what to get, and by what actions: how soon time will cover and bury all things, and how many it hath already buried!

THE SEVENTH BOOK

I. What is wickedness? It is that which many time and often thou hast already seen and known in the world. And so oft as anything doth happen that might otherwise trouble thee, let this memento presently come to thy mind, that it is that which thou hast already often Seen and known. Generally, above and below, thou shalt find but the same things. The very same things whereof ancient stories, middle age stories, and fresh stories are full whereof towns are full, and houses full. There is nothing that is new. All things that are, are both usual and of little continuance.

II. What fear is there that thy dogmata, or philosophical resolutions and conclusions, should become dead in thee, and lose their proper power and efficacy to make thee live happy, as long as those proper and correlative fancies, and representations of things on which they mutually depend (which continually to stir up and revive is in thy power,) are still kept fresh and alive? It is in my power concerning this thing that is happened, what soever it be, to conceit that which is right and true. If it be, why then am I troubled? Those things that are without my understanding, are nothing to it at all: and that is it only, which doth properly concern me. Be always in this mind, and thou wilt be right.

III. That which most men would think themselves most happy for, and would prefer before all things, if the Gods would grant it unto them after their deaths, thou mayst whilst thou livest grant unto thyself; to live again. See the things of the world again, as thou hast already seen them. For what is it else to live again? Public shows and solemnities with much pomp and vanity, stage plays, flocks and herds; conflicts and contentions: a bone thrown to a company of hungry curs; a bait for greedy fishes; the painfulness, and continual burden-bearing of wretched ants, the running to and fro of terrified mice: little puppets drawn up and down with wires and nerves: these be the objects of the world among all these thou must stand steadfast, meekly affected, and free from all manner of indignation; with this right ratiocination and apprehension; that as the worth is of those things which a man doth affect, so is in very deed every man's worth more or less.

IV. Word after word, every one by itself, must the things that are spoken be conceived and understood; and so the things that are done, purpose after purpose, every one by itself likewise. And as in matter of purposes and actions, we must presently see what is the proper use and relation of every one; so of words must we be as ready, to consider of every one what is the true meaning, and signification of it according to truth and nature, however it be taken in common use.

V. Is my reason, and understanding sufficient for this, or no? If it be sufficient, without any private applause, or public ostentation as of an instrument, which by nature I am provided of, I will make use of it for the work in hand, as of an instrument, which by nature I am provided of. if it be not, and that otherwise it belong not unto me particularly as a private duty, I will either give it over, and leave it to some other that can better effect it: or I will endeavour it; but with the help of some other, who with the joint help of my reason, is able to bring somewhat to pass, that will now be seasonable and useful for the common good. For whatsoever I do either by myself, or with some other, the only thing that I must intend, is, that it be good and expedient for the public. For as for praise, consider how many who once were much commended, are now already quite forgotten, yea they that commended them, how even they themselves are long since dead and gone. Be not therefore ashamed, whensoever thou must use the help of others. For whatsoever it be that lieth upon thee to effect, thou must propose it unto thyself, as the scaling of walls is unto a soldier. And what if thou through either lameness or some other impediment art not able to reach unto the top of the battlements alone, which with the help of another thou mayst; wilt thou therefore give it over, or go about it with less courage and alacrity, because thou canst not effect it all alone?

VI. Let not things future trouble thee. For if necessity so require that they come to pass, thou shalt (whensoever that is) be provided for them with the same reason, by which whatsoever is now present, is made both tolerable and acceptable unto thee. All things are linked and knitted together, and the knot is sacred, neither is there anything in the world, that is not kind and natural in regard of any other thing, or, that hath not some kind of reference and natural correspondence with whatsoever is in the world besides. For all things are ranked together, and by that decency of its due place and order that each particular doth observe, they all concur together to the making of one and the same κόσμος or world: as if you said, a comely piece, or an orderly composition. For all things throughout, there is but one and the same order; and through all things, one and the same God, the same substance and the same law. There is one common reason, and one common truth, that belongs unto all reasonable creatures, for neither is there save one perfection of all creatures that are of the same kind, and partakers of the same reason.

VII. Whatsoever is material, doth soon vanish away into the common substance of the whole; and whatsoever is formal, or, whatsoever doth animate that which is material, is soon resumed into the common reason of the whole; and the fame and memory of anything, is soon swallowed up by the general age and duration of the whole.

VIII. To a reasonable creature, the same action is both according to nature, and according to reason.

IX. Straight of itself, not made straight.

X. As several members in one body united, so are reasonable creatures in a body divided and dispersed, all made and prepared for one common operation. And this thou shalt apprehend the better, if thou shalt use thyself often to say to thyself, I am μέλος, or a member of the mass and body of reasonable substances. But if thou shalt say I am μέρος, or a part, thou dost not yet love men from thy heart. The joy that thou takest in the exercise of bounty, is not yet grounded upon a due ratiocination and right apprehension of the nature of things. Thou dost exercise it as yet upon this ground barely, as a thing convenient and fitting; not, as doing good to thyself, when thou dost good unto others.

XI. Of things that are external, happen what will to that which can suffer by external accidents. Those things that suffer let them complain themselves, if they will; as for me, as long as I conceive no such thing, that that which is happened is evil, I have no hurt; and it is in my power not to conceive any such thing.

XII. Whatsoever any man either doth or saith, thou must be good; not for any man's sake, but for thine own nature's sake; as if either gold, or the emerald, or purple, should ever be saying to themselves, Whatsoever any man either doth or saith, I must still be an emerald, and I must keep my colour.

XIII. This may ever be my comfort and security: my understanding, that ruleth over all, will not of itself bring trouble and vexation upon itself. This I say; it will not put itself in any fear, it will not lead itself into any concupiscence. If it be in the power of any other to compel it to fear, or to grieve, it is free for him to use his power. But sure if itself do not of itself, through some false opinion or supposition incline itself to any such disposition; there is no fear. For as for the body, why should I make the grief of my body, to be the grief of my mind? If that itself can either fear or complain, let it. But as for the soul, which indeed, can only be truly sensible of either fear or grief; to which only it belongs according to its different imaginations and opinions, to admit of either of these, or of their contraries; thou mayst look to that thyself, that it suffer nothing. Induce her not to any such opinion or persuasion. The understanding is of itself sufficient unto itself, and needs not (if itself doth not bring itself to need) any other thing besides itself, and by consequent as it needs nothing, so neither can it be troubled or hindered by anything, if itself doth not trouble and hinder itself.

XIV. What is εὐδαιμονία, or happiness: but ἀγαθὸς δαίμων, or, a good dæmon, or spirit? What then dost thou do here, O opinion? By the Gods I adjure thee, that thou get thee gone, as thou earnest: for I need thee not. Thou earnest indeed unto me according to thy ancient wonted manner. It is that, that all men have ever been subject unto. That thou camest therefore I am not angry with thee, only begone, now that I have found thee what thou art.

XV. Is any man so foolish as to fear change, to which all things that once were not owe their being? And what is it, that is more pleasing and more familiar to the nature of the universe? How couldst thou thyself use thy ordinary hot baths, should not the wood that heateth them first be changed? How couldst thou receive any nourishment from those things that thou hast eaten, if they should not be changed? Can anything else almost (that is useful and profitable) be brought to pass without change? How then dost not thou perceive, that for thee also, by death, to come to change, is a thing of the very same nature, and as necessary for the nature of the universe?

XVI. Through the substance of the universe, as through a torrent pass all particular bodies, being all of the same nature, and all joint workers with the universe itself as in one of our bodies so many members among themselves. How many such as Chrysippus, how many such as Socrates, how many such as Epictetus, hath the age of the world long since swallowed up and devoured? Let this, be it either men or businesses, that thou hast occasion to think of, to the end that thy thoughts be not distracted and thy mind too earnestly set upon anything, upon every such occasion presently come to thy mind. Of all my thoughts and cares, one only thing shall be the object, that I myself do nothing which to the proper constitution of man, (either in regard of the thing itself, or in regard of the manner, or of the time of doing,) is contrary. The time when thou shalt have forgotten all things, is at hand. And that time also is at hand, when thou thyself shalt be forgotten by all. Whilst thou art, apply thyself to that especially which unto man as he is a mart, is most proper and agreeable, and that is, for a man even to love them that transgress against him. This shall be, if at the same time that any such thing doth happen, thou call to mind, that they are thy kinsmen; that it is through ignorance and against their wills that they sin; and that within a very short while after, both thou and he shall be no more. But above all things, that he hath not done thee any hurt; for that by him thy mind and understanding is not made worse or more vile than it was before.

XVII. The nature of the universe, of the common substance of all things as it were of so much wax hath now perchance formed a horse; and then, destroying that figure, hath new tempered and fashioned the matter of it into the form and substance of a tree: then that again into the form and substance of a man: and then that again into some other. Now every one of these doth subsist but for a very little while. As for dissolution, if it be no grievous thing to the chest or trunk, to be joined together; why should it be more grievous to be put asunder?

XVIII. An angry countenance is much against nature, and it is oftentimes the proper countenance of them that are at the point of death. But were it so, that all anger and passion were so thoroughly quenched in thee, that it were altogether impossible to kindle it any more, yet herein must not thou rest satisfied, but further endeavour by good consequence of true ratiocination, perfectly to conceive and understand, that all anger and passion is against reason. For if thou shalt not be sensible of thine innocence; if that also shall be gone from thee, the comfort of a good conscience, that thou doest all things according to reason: what shouldest thou live any longer for? All things that now thou seest, are but for a moment. That nature, by which all things in the world are administered, will soon bring change and alteration upon them, and then of their substances make other things like unto them: and then soon after others again of the matter and substance of these: that so by these means, the world may still appear fresh and new.

XIX. Whensoever any man doth trespass against other, presently consider with thyself what it was that he did suppose to be good, what to be evil, when he did trespass. For this when thou knowest, thou wilt pity him thou wilt have no occasion either to wonder, or to be angry. For either thou thyself dust yet live in that error and ignorance, as that thou dust suppose either that very thing that he doth, or some other like worldly thing, to be good; and so thou art bound to pardon him if he have done that which thou in the like case wouldst have done thyself. Or if so be that thou dost not any more suppose the same things to be good or evil, that he doth; how canst thou but be gentle unto him that is in an error?

XX. Fancy not to thyself things future, as though they were present but of those that are present, take some aside, that thou takest most benefit of, and consider of them particularly, how wonderfully thou wouldst want them, if they were not present. But take heed withal, lest that whilst thou dust settle thy contentment in things present, thou grow in time so to overprize them, as that the want of them (whensoever it shall so fall out) should be a trouble and a vexation unto thee. Wind up thyself into thyself. Such is the nature of thy reasonable commanding part, as that if it exercise justice, and have by that means tranquillity within itself, it doth rest fully satisfied with itself without any other thing.

XXI. Wipe off all opinion stay the force and violence of unreasonable lusts and affections: circumscribe the present time examine whatsoever it be that is happened, either to thyself or to another: divide all present objects, either in that which is formal or material think of the last hour. That which thy neighbour hath committed, where the guilt of it lieth, there let it rest. Examine in order whatsoever is spoken. Let thy mind penetrate both into the effects, and into the causes. Rejoice thyself with true simplicity, and modesty; and that all middle things between virtue and vice are indifferent unto thee. Finally, love mankind; obey God.

XXII. All things (saith he) are by certain order and appointment. And what if the elements only.

It will suffice to remember, that all things in general are by certain order and appointment: or if it be but few. And as concerning death, that either dispersion, or the atoms, or annihilation, or extinction, or translation will ensue. And as concerning pain, that that which is intolerable is soon ended by death; and that which holds long must needs be tolerable; and that the mind in the meantime (which is all in all) may by way of interclusion, or interception, by stopping all manner of commerce and sympathy with the body, still retain its own tranquillity. Thy understanding is not made worse by it. As for those parts that suffer, let them, if they can, declare their grief themselves. As for praise and commendation, view their mind and understanding, what estate they are in; what kind of things they fly, and what things they seek after: and that as in the seaside, whatsoever was before to be seen, is by the continual succession of new heaps of sand cast up one upon another, soon hid and covered; so in this life, all former things by those which immediately succeed.

XXIII. Out of Plato. 'He then whose mind is endowed with true magnanimity, who hath accustomed himself to the contemplation both of all times, and of all things in general; can this mortal life (thinkest thou) seem any great matter unto him? It is not possible, answered he. Then neither will such a one account death a grievous thing? By no means.'

XXIV. Out of Antisthenes. 'It is a princely thing to do well, and to be ill-spoken of. It is a shameful thing that the face should be subject unto the mind, to be put into what shape it will, and to be dressed by it as it will; and that the mind should not bestow so much care upon herself, as to fashion herself, and to dress herself as best becometh her.'

XXV. Out of several poets and comics. 'It will but little avail thee, to turn thine anger and indignation upon the things themselves that have fallen across unto thee. For as for them, they are not sensible of it, &c. Thou shalt but make thyself a laughing-stock; both unto the Gods and men, &c. Our life is reaped like a ripe ear of corn; one is yet standing and another is down, &c. But if so be that I and my children be neglected by the gods, there is some reason even for that, &c. As long as right and equity is of my side, &c. Not to lament with them, not to tremble, &c.'

XXVI. Out of Plato. 'My answer, full of justice and equity, should be this: Thy speech is not right, O man! if thou supposest that he that is of any worth at all, should apprehend either life or death, as a matter of great hazard and danger; and should not make this rather his only care, to examine his own actions, whether just or unjust: whether actions of a good, or of a wicked man, &c. For thus in very truth stands the case, O ye men of Athens. What place or station soever a man either hath chosen to himself, judging it best for himself; or is by lawful authority put and settled in, therein do I think (all appearance of danger notwithstanding) that he should continue, as one who feareth neither death, nor anything else, so much as he feareth to commit anything that is vicious and shameful, &c. But, O noble sir, consider I pray, whether true generosity and true happiness, do not consist in somewhat else rather, than in the preservation either of our, or other men's lives. For it is not the part of a man that is a man indeed, to desire to live long or to make much of his life whilst he liveth: but rather (he that is such) will in these things wholly refer himself unto the Gods, and believing that which every woman can tell him, that no man can escape death; the only thing that he takes thought and care for is this, that what time he liveth, he may live as well and as virtuously as he can possibly, &c. To look about, and with the eyes to follow the course of the stars and planets as though thou wouldst run with them; and to mind perpetually the several changes of the elements one into another. For such fancies and imaginations, help much to purge away the dross and filth of this our earthly life,' &c. That also is a fine passage of Plato's, where he speaketh of worldly things in these words: 'Thou must also as from some higher place look down, as it were, upon the things of this world, as flocks, armies, husbandmen's labours, marriages, divorces, generations, deaths: the tumults of courts and places of judicatures; desert places; the several nations of barbarians, public festivals, mournings, fairs, markets.' How all things upon earth are pell-mell; and how miraculously things contrary one to another, concur to the beauty and perfection of this universe.

XXVII. To look back upon things of former ages, as upon the manifold changes and conversions of several monarchies and commonwealths. We may also foresee things future, for they shall all be of the same kind; neither is it possible that they should leave the tune, or break the concert that is now begun, as it were, by these things that are now done and brought to pass in the world. It comes all to one therefore, whether a man be a spectator of the things of this life but forty years, or whether he see them ten thousand years together: for what shall he see more? 'And as for those parts that came from the earth, they shall return unto the earth again; and those that came from heaven, they also shall return unto those heavenly places.' Whether it be a mere dissolution and unbinding of the manifold intricacies and entanglements of the confused atoms; or some such dispersion of the simple and incorruptible elements... 'With meats and drinks and divers charms, they seek to divert the channel, that they might not die. Yet must we needs endure that blast of wind that cometh from above, though we toil and labour never so much.'

XXVIII. He hath a stronger body, and is a better wrestler than I. What then? Is he more bountiful? is he more modest? Doth he bear all adverse chances with more equanimity: or with his neighbour's offences with more meekness and gentleness than I?

XXIX. Where the matter may be effected agreeably to that reason, which both unto the Gods and men is common, there can be no just cause of grief or sorrow. For where the fruit and benefit of an action well begun and prosecuted according to the proper constitution of man may be reaped and obtained, or is sure and certain, it is against reason that any damage should there be suspected. In all places, and at all times, it is in thy power religiously to embrace whatsoever by God's appointment is happened unto thee, and justly to converse with those men, whom thou hast to do with, and accurately to examine every fancy that presents itself, that nothing may slip and steal in, before thou hast rightly apprehended the true nature of it.

XXX. Look not about upon other men's minds and understandings; but look right on forwards whither nature, both that of the universe, in those things that happen unto thee; and thine in particular, in those things that are done by thee: doth lead, and direct thee. Now every one is bound to do that, which is consequent and agreeable to that end which by his true natural constitution he was ordained unto. As for all other things, they are ordained for the use of reasonable creatures: as in all things we see that that which is worse and inferior, is made for that which is better. Reasonable creatures, they are ordained one for another. That therefore which is chief in every man's constitution, is, that he intend the common good. The second is, that he yield not to any lusts and motions of the flesh. For it is the part and privilege of the reasonable and intellective faculty, that she can so bound herself, as that neither the sensitive, nor the appetitive faculties, may not anyways prevail upon her. For both these are brutish. And therefore over both she challengeth mastery, and cannot anyways endure, if in her right temper, to be subject unto either. And this indeed most justly. For by nature she was ordained to command all in the body. The third thing proper to man by his constitution, is, to avoid all rashness and precipitancy; and not to be subject to error. To these things then, let the mind apply herself and go straight on, without any distraction about other things, and she hath her end, and by consequent her happiness.

XXXI. As one who had lived, and were now to die by right, whatsoever is yet remaining, bestow that wholly as a gracious overplus upon a virtuous life. Love and affect that only, whatsoever it be that happeneth, and is by the fates appointed unto thee. For what can be more reasonable? And as anything doth happen unto thee by way of cross, or calamity, call to mind presently and set before thine eyes, the examples of some other men, to whom the self-same thing did once happen likewise. Well, what did they? They grieved; they wondered; they complained. And where are they now? All dead and gone. Wilt thou also be like one of them? Or rather leaving to men of the world (whose life both in regard of themselves, and them that they converse with, is nothing but mere mutability; or men of as fickle minds, as fickle bodies; ever changing and soon changed themselves) let it be thine only care and study, how to make a right use of all such accidents. For there is good use to be made of them, and they will prove fit matter for thee to work upon, if it shall be both thy care and thy desire, that whatsoever thou doest, thou thyself mayst like and approve thyself for it. And both these, see, that thou remember well, according as the diversity of the matter of the action that of soul Socrates had: whether his disposition was such; as that all that he stood upon, and sought after in this world, was barely this, that he might ever carry himself justly towards men, and holily towards the Gods. Neither vexing himself to no purpose at the wickedness of others, nor yet ever condescending to any man's evil fact, or evil intentions, through either fear, or engagement of friendship. Whether of those things that happened unto him by God's appointment, he neither did wonder at any when it did happen, or thought it intolerable in the trial of it. And lastly, whether he never did suffer his mind to sympathise with the senses, and affections of the body. For we must not think that Nature hath so mixed and tempered it with the body, as that she hath not power to circumscribe herself, and by herself to intend her own ends and occasions.

XXXVIII. For it is a thing very possible, that a man should be a very divine man, and yet be altogether unknown. This thou must ever be mindful of, as of this also, that a man's true happiness doth consist in very few things. And that although thou dost despair, that thou shalt ever be a good either logician, or naturalist, yet thou art never the further off by it from being either liberal, or modest, or charitable, or obedient unto God.

XXXIX. Free from all compulsion in all cheerfulness and alacrity thou mayst run out thy time, though men should exclaim against thee never so much, and the wild beasts should pull in sunder the poor members of thy pampered mass of flesh. For what in either of these or the like cases should hinder the mind to retain her own rest and tranquillity, consisting both in the right judgment of those things that happen unto her, and in the ready use of all present matters and occasions? So that her judgment may say, to that which is befallen her by way of cross: this thou art in very deed, and according to thy true nature: notwithstanding that in the judgment of opinion thou dust appear otherwise: and her discretion to the present object; thou art that, which I sought for. For whatsoever it be, that is now present, shall ever be embraced by me as a fit and seasonable object, both for my reasonable faculty, and for my sociable, or charitable inclination to work upon. And that which is principal in this matter, is that it may be referred either unto the praise of God, or to the good of men. For either unto God or man, whatsoever it is that doth happen in the world hath in the ordinary course of nature its proper reference; neither is there anything, that in regard of nature is either new, or reluctant and intractable, but all things both usual and easy.

XL. Then hath a man attained to the estate of perfection in his life and conversation, when he so spends every day, as if it were his last day: never hot and vehement in his affections, nor yet so cold and stupid as one that had no sense; and free from all manner of dissimulation.

XLI. Can the Gods, who are immortal, for the continuance of so many ages bear without indignation with such and so many sinners, as have ever been, yea not only so, but also take such care for them, that they want nothing; and dust thou so grievously take on, as one that could bear with them no longer; thou that art but for a moment of time? yea thou that art one of those sinners thyself? A very ridiculous thing it is, that any man should dispense with vice and wickedness in himself, which is in his power to restrain; and should go about to suppress it in others, which is altogether impossible.

XLII. What object soever, our reasonable and sociable faculty doth meet with, that affords nothing either for the satisfaction of reason, or for the practice of charity, she worthily doth think unworthy of herself.

XLIII. When thou hast done well, and another is benefited by thy action, must thou like a very fool look for a third thing besides, as that it may appear unto others also that thou hast done well, or that thou mayest in time, receive one good turn for another? No man useth to be weary of that which is beneficial unto him. But every action according to nature, is beneficial. Be not weary then of doing that which is beneficial unto thee, whilst it is so unto others.

XLIV. The nature of the universe did once certainly before it was created, whatsoever it hath done since, deliberate and so resolve upon the creation of the world. Now since that time, whatsoever it is, that is and happens in the world, is either but a consequent of that one and first deliberation: or if so be that this ruling rational part of the world, takes any thought and care of things particular, they are surely his reasonable and principal creatures, that are the proper object of his particular care and providence. This often thought upon, will much conduce to thy tranquillity.

THE EIGHTH BOOK

I. This also, among other things, may serve to keep thee from vainglory; if thou shalt consider, that thou art now altogether incapable of the commendation of one, who all his life long, or from his youth at least, hath lived a philosopher's life. For both unto others, and to thyself especially, it is well known, that thou hast done many things contrary to that perfection of life. Thou hast therefore been confounded in thy course, and henceforth it will be hard for thee to recover the title and credit of a philosopher. And to it also is thy calling and profession repugnant. If therefore thou dost truly understand, what it is that is of moment indeed; as for thy fame and credit, take no thought or care for that: let it suffice thee if all the rest of thy life, be it more or less, thou shalt live as thy nature requireth, or according to the true and natural end of thy making. Take pains therefore to know what it is that thy nature requireth, and let nothing else distract thee. Thou hast already had sufficient experience, that of those many things that hitherto thou hast erred and wandered about, thou couldst not find happiness in any of them. Not in syllogisms, and logical subtilties, not in wealth, not in honour and reputation, not in pleasure. In none of all these. Wherein then is it to be found? In the practice of those things, which the nature of man, as he is a man, doth require. How then shall he do those things? if his dogmata, or moral tenets and opinions (from which all motions and actions do proceed), be right and true. Which be those dogmata? Those that concern that which is good or evil, as that there is nothing truly good and beneficial unto man, but that which makes him just, temperate, courageous, liberal; and that there is nothing truly evil and hurtful unto man, but that which causeth the contrary effects.

II. Upon every action that thou art about, put this question to thyself; How will this when it is done agree with me? Shall I have no occasion to repent of it? Yet a very little while and I am dead and gone; and all things are at end. What then do I care for more than this, that my present action whatsoever it be, may be the proper action of one that is reasonable; whose end is, the common good; who in all things is ruled and governed by the same law of right and reason, by which God Himself is.

III. Alexander, Caius, Pompeius; what are these to Diogenes, Heraclitus, and Socrates? These penetrated into the true nature of things; into all causes, and all subjects: and upon these did they exercise their power and authority. But as for those, as the extent of their error was, so far did their slavery extend.

IV. What they have done, they will still do, although thou shouldst hang thyself. First; let it not trouble thee. For all things both good and evil: come to pass according to the nature and general condition of the universe, and within a very little while, all things will be at an end; no man will be remembered: as now of Africanus (for example) and Augustus it is already come to pass. Then secondly; fix thy mind upon the thing itself; look into it, and remembering thyself, that thou art bound nevertheless to be a good man, and what it is that thy nature requireth of thee as thou art a man, be not diverted from what thou art about, and speak that which seemeth unto thee most just: only speak it kindly, modestly, and without hypocrisy.

V. That which the nature of the universe doth busy herself about, is; that which is here, to transfer it thither, to change it, and thence again to take it away, and to carry it to another place. So that thou needest not fear any new thing. For all things are usual and ordinary; and all things are disposed by equality.

VI. Every particular nature hath content, when in its own proper course it speeds. A reasonable nature doth then speed, when first in matter of fancies and imaginations, it gives no consent to that which is either false uncertain. Secondly, when in all its motions and resolutions it takes its level at the common good only, and that it desireth nothing, and flieth from nothing, bet what is in its own power to compass or avoid. And lastly, when it willingly and gladly embraceth, whatsoever is dealt and appointed unto it by the common nature. For it is part of it; even as the nature of any one leaf, is part of the common nature of all plants and trees. But that the nature of a leaf, is part of a nature both unreasonable and unsensible, and which in its proper end may be hindered; or, which is servile and slavish: whereas the nature of man is part of a common nature which cannot be hindered, and which is both reasonable and just. From whence also it is, that according to the worth of everything, she doth make such equal distribution of all things, as of duration, substance form, operation, and of events and accidents. But herein consider not whether thou shalt find this equality in everything absolutely and by itself; but whether in all the particulars of some one thing taken together, and compared with all the particulars of some other thing, and them together likewise.

VII. Thou hast no time nor opportunity to read. What then? Hast thou not time and opportunity to exercise thyself, not to wrong thyself; to strive against all carnal pleasures and pains, and to get the upper hand of them; to contemn honour and vainglory; and not only, not to be angry with them, whom towards thee thou doest find unsensible and unthankful; but also to have a care of them still, and of their welfare?

VIII. Forbear henceforth to complain of the trouble of a courtly life, either in public before others, or in private by thyself.

IX. Repentance is an inward and self-reprehension for the neglect or omission of somewhat that was profitable. Now whatsoever is good, is also profitable, and it is the part of an honest virtuous man to set by it, and to make reckoning of it accordingly. But never did any honest virtuous man repent of the neglect or omission of any carnal pleasure: no carnal pleasure then is either good or profitable.

X. This, what is it in itself, and by itself, according to its proper constitution? What is the substance of it? What is the matter, or proper use? What is the form or efficient cause? What is it for in this world, and how long will it abide? Thus must thou examine all things, that present themselves unto thee.

XI. When thou art hard to be stirred up and awaked out of thy sleep, admonish thyself and call to mind, that, to perform actions tending to the common good is that which thine own proper constitution, and that which the nature of man do require. But to sleep, is common to unreasonable creatures also. And what more proper and natural, yea what more kind and pleasing, than that which is according to nature?

XII. As every fancy and imagination presents itself unto thee, consider (if it be possible) the true nature, and the proper qualities of it, and reason with thyself about it.

XIII. At thy first encounter with any one, say presently to thyself: This man, what are his opinions concerning that which is good or evil? as concerning pain, pleasure, and the causes of both; concerning honour, and dishonour, concerning life and death? thus and thus. Now if it be no wonder that a man should have such and such opinions, how can it be a wonder that he should do such and such things? I will remember then, that he cannot but do as he doth, holding those opinions that he doth. Remember, that as it is a shame for any man to wonder that a fig tree should bear figs, so also to wonder that the world should bear anything, whatsoever it is which in the ordinary course of nature it may bear. To a physician also and to a pilot it is a shame either for the one to wonder, that such and such a one should have an ague; or for the other, that the winds should prove Contrary.

XIV. Remember, that to change thy mind upon occasion, and to follow him that is able to rectify thee, is equally ingenuous, as to find out at the first, what is right and just, without help. For of thee nothing is required, ti, is beyond the extent of thine own deliberation and jun. merit, and of thine own understanding.

XV. If it were thine act and in thine own power, wouldest thou do it? If it were not, whom dost tin accuse?

the atoms, or the Gods? For to do either, the part of a mad man. Thou must therefore blame nobody, but if it be in thy power, redress what is amiss; if it be not, to what end is it to complain? For nothing should be done but to some certain end.

XVI. Whatsoever dieth and falleth, however and wheresoever it die and fall, it cannot fall out of the world, here it have its abode and change, here also shall it have its dissolution into its proper elements. The same are the world's elements, and the elements of which thou dost consist. And they when they are changed, they murmur not; why shouldest thou?

XVII. Whatsoever is, was made for something: as a horse, a vine. Why wonderest thou? The sun itself will say of itself, I was made for something; and so hath every god its proper function. What then were then made for? to disport and delight thyself? See how even common sense and reason cannot brook it.

XVIII. Nature hath its end as well in the end and final consummation of anything that is, as in the begin-nine and continuation of it.

XIX. As one that tosseth up a ball. And what is a ball the better, if the motion of it be upwards; or the worse if it be downwards; or if it chance to fall upon the ground? So for the bubble; if it continue, what it the better? and if it dissolve, what is it the worse And so is it of a candle too. And so must thou reason with thyself, both in matter of fame, and in matter of death. For as for the body itself, (the subject of death) wouldest thou know the vileness of it? Turn it about that thou mayest behold it the worst sides upwards as well, as in its more ordinary pleasant shape; how doth it look, when it is old and withered? when sick and pained? when in the act of lust, and fornication? And as for fame. This life is short. Both he that praiseth, and he that is praised; he that remembers, and he that is remembered, will soon be dust and ashes. Besides, it is but in one corner of this part of the world that thou art praised; and yet in this corner, thou hast not the joint praises of all men; no nor scarce of any one constantly. And yet the whole earth itself, what is it but as one point, in regard of the whole world?

XX. That which must be the subject of thy consideration, is either the matter itself, or the dogma, or the operation, or the true sense and signification.

XXI. Most justly have these things happened unto thee: why dost not thou amend? O but thou hadst rather become good to-morrow, than to be so to-day.

XXII. Shall I do it? I will; so the end of my action be to do good unto men. Doth anything by way of cross or adversity happen unto me? I accept it, with reference unto the Gods, and their providence; the fountain of all things, from which whatsoever comes to pass, doth hang and depend.

XXIII. By one action judge of the rest: this bathing which usually takes up so much of our time, what is it? Oil, sweat, filth; or the sordes of the body: an excrementitious viscosity, the excrements of oil and other ointments used about the body, and mixed with the sordes of the body: all base and loathsome. And such almost is every part of our life; and every worldly object.

XXIV. Lucilla buried Verus; then was Lucilla herself buried by others. So Secunda Maximus, then Secunda herself. So Epitynchanus, Diotimus; then Epitynchanus himself. So Antoninus Pius, Faustina his wife; then Antoninus himself. This is the course of the world. First Celer, Adrianus; then Adrianus himself. And those austere ones; those that foretold other men's deaths; those that were so proud and stately, where are they now? Those austere ones I mean, such as were Charax, and Demetrius the Platonic, and Eudaemon, and others like unto those. They were all but for one day; all dead and gone long since. Some of them no sooner dead, than forgotten. Others soon turned into fables. Of others, even that which was fabulous, is now long since forgotten. This thereafter thou must remember, that whatsoever thou art compounded of, shall soon be dispersed, and that thy life and breath, or thy soul, shall either be no more or shall ranslated (sp.), and appointed to some certain place and station.

XXV. The true joy of a man, is to do that which properly belongs unto a man. That which is most proper unto a man, is, first, to be kindly affected towards them that are of the same kind and nature as he is himself to contemn all sensual motions and appetites, to discern rightly all plausible fancies and imaginations, to contemplate the nature of the universe; both it, and things that are done in it. In which kind of contemplation three several relations are to be observed The first, to the apparent secondary cause. The Second to the first original cause, God, from whom originally proceeds whatsoever doth happen in the world. The third and last, to them that we live and converse with: what use may be made of it, to their use and benefit.

XXVI. If pain be an evil, either it is in regard of the body; (and that cannot be, because the body of itself is altogether insensible:) or in regard of the soul But it is in the power of the soul, to preserve her own peace and tranquillity, and not to suppose that pain is evil. For all judgment and deliberation; all prosecution, or aversation is from within, whither the sense of evil (except it be let in by opinion) cannot penetrate.

XXVII. Wipe off all idle fancies, and say unto thyself incessantly; Now if I will, it is in my power to keep out of this my soul all wickedness, all lust, and concupiscences, all trouble and confusion. But on the contrary to behold and consider all things according to their true nature, and to carry myself towards everything according to its true worth. Remember then this thy power that nature hath given thee.

XXVIII. Whether thou speak in the Senate or whether thou speak to any particular, let thy speech In always grave and modest. But thou must not openly and vulgarly observe that sound and exact form of speaking, concerning that which is truly good and truly civil; the vanity of the world, and of worldly men: which otherwise truth and reason doth prescribe.

XXIX. Augustus his court; his wife, his daughter, his nephews, his sons-in-law his sister, Agrippa, his kinsmen, his domestics, his friends; Areus, Mæcenas, his slayers of beasts for sacrifice and divination: there thou hast the death of a whole court together. Proceed now on to the rest that have been since that of Augustus. Hath death dwelt with them otherwise, though so many and so stately whilst they lived, than it doth use to deal with any one particular man? Consider now the death of a whole kindred and family, as of that of the Pompeys, as that also that useth to be written upon some monuments, HE WAS THE LAST OF HIS OWN KINDRED. O what care did his predecessors take, that they might leave a successor, yet behold at last one or other must of necessity be THE LAST. Here again therefore consider the death of a whole kindred.

XXX. Contract thy whole life to the measure and proportion of one single action. And if in every particular action thou dost perform what is fitting to the utmost of thy power, let it suffice thee. And who can hinder thee, but that thou mayest perform what is fitting? But there may be some outward let and impediment. Not any, that can hinder thee, but that whatsoever thou dost, thou may do it, justly, temperately, and with the praise of God. Yea, but there may be somewhat, whereby some operation or other of thine may be hindered. And then, with that very thing that doth hinder, thou mayest he well pleased, and so by this gentle and equanimious conversion of thy mind unto that which may be, instead of that which at first thou didst intend, in the room of that former action there succeedeth another, which agrees as well with this contraction of thy life, that we now speak of.

XXXI. Receive temporal blessings without ostentation, when they are sent and thou shalt be able to part with them with all readiness and facility when they are taken from thee again.

XXXII. If ever thou sawest either a hand, or a foot, or a head lying by itself, in some place or other, as cut off from the rest of the body, such must thou conceive him to make himself, as much as in him lieth, that either is offended with anything that is happened, (whatsoever it be) and as it were divides himself from it: or that commits anything against the natural law of mutual correspondence, and society among men: or, he that, commits any act of uncharitableness. Whosoever thou art, thou art such, thou art cast forth I know not whither out of the general unity, which is according to nature. Thou went born indeed a part, but now thou hast cut thyself off. However, herein is matter of joy and exultation, that thou mayst be united again. God hath not granted it unto any other part, that once separated and cut off, it might be reunited, and come together again. But, behold, that GOODNESS how great and immense it is! which hath so much esteemed MAN. As at first he was so made, that he needed not, except he would himself, have divided himself from the whole; so once divided and cut off, IT hath so provided and ordered it, that if he would himself, he might return, and grow together again, and be admitted into its former rank and place of a part, as he was before.

XXXIII. As almost all her other faculties and properties the nature of the universe hath imparted unto every reasonable creature, so this in particular we have received from her, that as whatsoever doth oppose itself unto her, and doth withstand her in her purposes and intentions, she doth, though against its will and intention, bring it about to herself, to serve herself of it in the execution of her own destinated ends; and so by this though not intended co-operation of it with herself makes it part of herself whether it will or no. So may every reasonable creature, what crosses and impediments soever it meets with in the course of this mortal life, it may use them as fit and proper objects, to the furtherance of whatsoever it intended and absolutely proposed unto itself as its natural end and happiness.

XXXIV. Let not the general representation unto thyself of the wretchedness of this our mortal life, trouble thee. Let not thy mind wander up and down, and heap together in her thoughts the many troubles and grievous calamities which thou art as subject unto as any other. But as everything in particular doth happen, put this question unto thyself, and say: What is it that in this present matter, seems unto thee so intolerable? For thou wilt be ashamed to confess it. Then upon this presently call to mind, that neither that which is future, nor that which is past can hurt thee; but that only which is present. (And that also is much lessened, if thou dost lightly circumscribe it:) and then check thy mind if for so little a while, (a mere instant), it cannot hold out with patience.

XXXV. What? are either Panthea or Pergamus abiding to this day by their masters' tombs? or either Chabrias or Diotimus by that of Adrianus? O foolery! For what if they did, would their masters be sensible of It? or if sensible, would they be glad of it? or if glad, were these immortal? Was not it appointed unto them also (both men and women,) to become old in time, and then to die? And these once dead, what would become of these former? And when all is done, what is all this for, but for a mere bag of blood and corruption?

XXXVI. If thou beest quick-sighted, be so in matter of judgment, and best discretion, saith he.

XXXVII. In the whole constitution of man, I see not any virtue contrary to justice, whereby it may be resisted and opposed. But one whereby pleasure and voluptuousness may be resisted and opposed, I see: continence.

XXXVIII. If thou canst but withdraw conceit and opinion concerning that which may seem hurtful and offensive, thou thyself art as safe, as safe may be. Thou thyself? and who is that? Thy reason. 'Yea, but I am not reason.' Well, be it so. However, let not thy reason or understanding admit of grief, and if there be anything in thee that is grieved, let that, (whatsoever it be,) conceive its own grief, if it can.

XXXIX. That which is a hindrance of the senses, is an evil to the sensitive nature. That which is a hindrance of the appetitive and prosecutive faculty, is an evil to the sensitive nature. As of the sensitive, so of the vegetative constitution, whatsoever is a hindrance unto it, is also in that respect an evil unto the same. And so likewise, whatsoever is a hindrance unto the mind and understanding, must needs be the proper evil of the reasonable nature. Now apply all those things unto thyself. Do either pain or pleasure seize on thee? Let the senses look to that. Hast thou met with Some obstacle or other in thy purpose and intention? If thou didst propose without due reservation and exception now hath thy reasonable part received a blow indeed But if in general thou didst propose unto thyself what soever might be, thou art not thereby either hurt, nor properly hindered. For in those things that properly belong unto the mind, she cannot be hindered by any man. It is not fire, nor iron; nor the power of a tyrant nor the power of a slandering tongue; nor anything else that can penetrate into her.

XL. If once round and solid, there is no fear that ever it will change. XLI. Why should I grieve myself; who never did willingly grieve any other! One thing rejoices one and another thing another. As for me, this is my joy, if my understanding be right and sound, as neither averse from any man, nor refusing any of those things which as a man I am subject unto; if I can look upon all things in the world meekly and kindly; accept all things and carry myself towards everything according to to true worth of the thing itself.

XLII. This time that is now present, bestow thou upon thyself. They that rather hunt for fame after death, do not consider, that those men that shall be hereafter, will be even such, as these whom now they can so hardly bear with. And besides they also will be mortal men. But to consider the thing in itself, if so many with so many voices, shall make such and such a sound, or shall have such and such an opinion concerning thee, what is it to thee?

XLIII. Take me and throw me where thou wilt: I am indifferent. For there also I shall have that spirit which is within me propitious; that is well pleased and fully contented both in that constant disposition, and with those particular actions, which to its own proper constitution are suitable and agreeable.

XLIV. Is this then a thing of that worth, that for it my soul should suffer, and become worse than it was? as either basely dejected, or disordinately affected, or confounded within itself, or terrified? What can there be, that thou shouldest so much esteem?

XLV. Nothing can happen unto thee, which is not incidental unto thee, as thou art a man. As nothing can happen either to an ox, a vine, or to a stone, which is not incidental unto them; unto every one in his own kind. If therefore nothing can happen unto anything, which is not both usual and natural; why art thou displeased? Sure the common nature of all would not bring anything upon any, that were intolerable. If therefore it be a thing external that causes thy grief, know, that it is not that properly that doth cause it, but thine own conceit and opinion concerning the thing: which thou mayest rid thyself of, when thou wilt. But if it be somewhat that is amiss in thine own disposition, that doth grieve thee, mayest thou not rectify thy moral tenets and opinions. But if it grieve thee, that thou doest not perform that which seemeth unto thee right and just, why doest not thou choose rather to perform it than to grieve? But somewhat that is stronger than thyself doth hinder thee. Let it not grieve thee then, if it be not thy fault that the thing is not performed. 'Yea but it is a thing of that nature, as that thy life is not worth the while, except it may be performed.' If it be so, upon condition that thou be kindly and lovingly disposed towards all men, thou mayest be gone. For even then, as much as at any time, art thou in a very good estate of performance, when thou doest die in charity with those, that are an obstacle unto thy performance.

XLVI. Remember that thy mind is of that nature as that it becometh altogether unconquerable, when once recollected in herself, she seeks no other content than this, that she cannot be forced: yea though it so fall out, that it be even against reason itself, that it cloth bandy. How much less when by the help of reason she is able to judge of things with discretion? And therefore let thy chief fort and place of defence be, a mind free from passions. A stronger place, (whereunto to make his refuge, and so to become impregnable) and better fortified than this, hath no man. He that seeth not this is unlearned. He that seeth it, and betaketh not himself to this place of refuge, is unhappy.

XLVII. Keep thyself to the first bare and naked apprehensions of things, as they present themselves unto thee, and add not unto them. It is reported unto thee, that such a one speaketh ill of thee. Well; that he speaketh ill of thee, so much is reported. But that thou art hurt thereby, is not reported: that is the addition of opinion, which thou must exclude. I see that my child is sick. That he is sick, I see, but that he is in danger of his life also, I see it not. Thus thou must use to keep thyself to the first motions and apprehensions of things, as they present themselves outwardly; and add not unto them from within thyself through mere conceit and opinion. Or rather add unto them: hut as one that understandeth the true nature of all things that happen in the world.

XLVIII. Is the cucumber bitter? set it away. Brambles are in the way? avoid them. Let this suffice. Add not presently speaking unto thyself, What serve these things for in the world? For, this, one that is acquainted with the mysteries of nature, will laugh at thee for it; as a carpenter would or a shoemaker, if meeting in either of their shops with some shavings, or small remnants of their work, thou shouldest blame them for it. And yet those men, it is not for want of a place where to throw them that they keep them in their shops for a while: but the nature of the universe hath no such out-place; but herein doth consist the wonder of her art and skill, that she having once circumscribed herself within some certain bounds and limits, whatsoever is within her that seems either corrupted, or old, or unprofitable, she can change it into herself, and of these very things can make new things; so that she needeth not to seek elsewhere out of herself either for a new supply of matter and substance, or for a place where to throw out whatsoever is irrecoverably putrid and corrupt. Thus she, as for place, so for matter and art, is herself sufficient unto herself.

XLIX. Not to be slack and negligent; or loose, and wanton in thy actions; nor contentious, and troublesome in thy conversation; nor to rove and wander in thy fancies and imaginations. Not basely to contract thy soul; nor boisterously to sally out with it, or furiously to launch out as it were, nor ever to want employment.

L. 'They kill me, they cut my flesh; they persecute my person with curses.' What then? May not thy mind for all this continue pure, prudent, temperate, just? As a fountain of sweet and clear water, though she be cursed by some stander by, yet do her springs nevertheless still run as sweet and clear as before; yea though either dirt or dung be thrown in, yet is it no sooner thrown, than dispersed, and she cleared. She cannot be dyed or infected by it. What then must I do, that I may have within myself an overflowing fountain, and not a well? Beget thyself by continual pains and endeavours to true liberty with charity, and true simplicity and modesty.

LI. He that knoweth not what the world is, knoweth not where he himself is. And he that knoweth not what the world was made for, cannot possibly know either what are the qualities, or what is the nature of the world. Now he that in either of these is to seek, for what he himself was made is ignorant also. What then dost thou think of that man, who proposeth unto himself, as a matter of great moment, the noise and applause of men, who both where they are, and what they are themselves, are altogether ignorant? Dost thou desire to be commended of that man, who thrice in one hour perchance, doth himself curse himself? Dost thou desire to please him, who pleaseth not himself? or dost thou think that he pleaseth himself, who doth use to repent himself almost of everything that he doth?

LII. Not only now henceforth to have a common breath, or to hold correspondency of breath, with that air, that compasseth us about; but to have a common mind, or to hold correspondency of mind also with that rational substance, which compasseth all things. For, that also is of itself, and of its own nature (if a man can but draw it in as he should) everywhere diffused; and passeth through all things, no less than the air doth, if a man can but suck it in.

LIII. Wickedness in general doth not hurt the world. Particular wickedness doth not hurt any other: only unto him it is hurtful, whosoever he be that offends, unto whom in great favour and mercy it is granted, that whensoever he himself shall but first desire it, he may be presently delivered of it. Unto my free-will my neighbour's free-will, whoever he be, (as his life, or his bode), is altogether indifferent. For though we are all made one for another, yet have our minds and understandings each of them their own proper and limited jurisdiction. For else another man's wickedness might be my evil which God would not have, that it might not be in another man's power to make me unhappy: which nothing now can do but mine own wickedness.

LIV. The sun seemeth to be shed abroad. And indeed it is diffused but not effused. For that diffusion of it is a τάσις or an extension. For therefore are the beams of it called ἀκτῖνες from the word ἐκτείνεσθαι to be stretched out and extended. Now what a sunbeam is, thou mayest know if thou observe the light of the sun, when through some narrow hole it pierceth into some room that is dark. For it is always in a direct line. And as by any solid body, that it meets with in the way that is not penetrable by air, it is divided and abrupted, and yet neither slides off, or falls down, but stayeth there nevertheless: such must the diffusion in the mind be; not an effusion, but an extension. What obstacles and impediments soever she meeteth within her way, she must not violently, and by way of an impetuous onset light upon them; neither must she fall down; but she must stand, and give light unto that which doth admit of it. For as for that which doth not, it is its own fault and loss, if it bereave itself of her light.

LV. He that feareth death, either feareth that he shall have no sense at all, or that his senses will not be the same. Whereas, he should rather comfort himself, that either no sense at all, and so no sense of evil; or if any sense, then another life, and so no death properly.

LVI. All men are made one for another: either then teach them better, or bear with them.

LVII. The motion of the mind is not as the motion of a dart. For the mind when it is wary and cautelous, and by way of diligent circumspection turneth herself many ways, may then as well be said to go straight on to the object, as when it useth no such circumspection.

LVIII. To pierce and penetrate into the estate of every one's understanding that thou hast to do with: as also to make the estate of thine own open, and penetrable to any other.

THE NINTH BOOK

I. He that is unjust, is also impious. For the nature of the universe, having made all reasonable creatures one for another, to the end that they should do one another good; more or less according to the several persons and occasions but in nowise hurt one another: it is manifest that he that doth transgress against this her will, is guilty of impiety towards the most ancient and venerable of all the deities. For the nature of the universe, is the nature the common parent of all, and therefore piously to be observed of all things that are, and that which now is, to whatsoever first was, and gave it its being, hath relation of blood and kindred. She is also called truth and is the first cause of all truths. He therefore that willingly and wittingly doth lie, is impious in that he doth receive, and so commit injustice: but he that against his will, in that he disagreeth from the nature of the universe, and in that striving with the nature of the world he doth in his particular, violate the general order of the world. For he doth no better than strive and war against it, who contrary to his own nature applieth himself to that which is contrary to truth. For nature had before furnished him with instincts and opportunities sufficient for the attainment of it; which he having hitherto neglected, is not now able to discern that which is false from that which is true. He also that pursues after pleasures, as that which is truly good and flies from pains, as that which is truly evil: is impious. For such a one must of necessity oftentimes accuse that common nature, as distributing many things both unto the evil, and unto the good, not according to the deserts of either: as unto the bad oftentimes pleasures, and the causes of pleasures; so unto the good, pains, and the occasions of pains. Again, he that feareth pains and crosses in this world, feareth some of those things which some time or other must needs happen in the world. And that we have already showed to be impious. And he that pursueth after pleasures, will not spare, to compass his desires, to do that which is unjust, and that is manifestly impious. Now those things which unto nature are equally indifferent (for she had not created both, both pain and pleasure, if both had not been unto her equally indifferent): they that will live according to nature, must in those things (as being of the same mind and disposition that she is) be as equally indifferent. Whosoever therefore in either matter of pleasure and pain; death and life; honour and dishonour, (which things nature in the administration of the world, indifferently doth make use of), is not as indifferent, it is apparent that he is impious. When I say that common nature doth indifferently make use of them, my meaning is, that they happen indifferently in the ordinary course of things, which by a necessary consequence, whether as principal or accessory, come to pass in the world, according to that first and ancient deliberation of Providence, by which she from some certain beginning, did resolve upon the creation of such a world, conceiving then in her womb as it were some certain rational generative seeds and faculties of things future, whether subjects, changes, successions; both such and such, and just so many.

II. It were indeed more happy and comfortable, for a man to depart out of this world, having lived all his life long clear from all falsehood, dissimulation, voluptuousness, and pride. But if this cannot be, yet it is some comfort for a man joyfully to depart as weary, and out of love with those; rather than to desire to live, and to continue long in those wicked courses. Hath not yet experience taught thee to fly from the plague? For a far greater plague is the corruption of the mind, than any certain change and distemper of the common air can be. This is a plague of creatures, as they are living creatures; but that of men as they are men or reasonable.

III. Thou must not in matter of death carry thyself scornfully, but as one that is well pleased with it, as being one of those things that nature hath appointed. For what thou dost conceive of these, of a boy to become a young man, to wax old, to grow, to ripen, to get teeth, or a beard, or grey hairs to beget, to bear, or to be delivered; or what other action soever it be, that is natural unto man according to the several seasons of his life; such a thing is it also to be dissolved. It is therefore the part of a wise man, in matter of death, not in any wise to carry himself either violently, or proudly but patiently to wait for it, as one of nature's operations: that with the same mind as now thou dost expect when that which yet is but an embryo in thy wife's belly shall come forth, thou mayst expect also when thy soul shall fall off from that outward coat or skin: wherein as a child in the belly it lieth involved and shut up. But thou desirest a more popular, and though not so direct and philosophical, yet a very powerful and penetrative recipe against the fear of death, nothing can make they more willing to part with thy life, than if thou shalt consider, both what the subjects themselves are that thou shalt part with, and what manner of disposition thou shalt no more have to do with. True it is, that, offended with them thou must not be by no means, but take care of them, and meekly bear with them However, this thou mayst remember, that whensoever it happens that thou depart, it shall not be from men that held the same opinions that thou dost. For that indeed, (if it were so) is the only thing that might make thee averse from death, and willing to continue here, if it were thy hap to live with men that had obtained the same belief that thou hast. But now, what a toil it is for thee to live with men of different opinions, thou seest: so that thou hast rather occasion to say, Hasten, I thee pray, O Death; lest I also in time forget myself.

IV. He that sinneth, sinneth unto himself. He that is unjust, hurts himself, in that he makes himself worse than he was before. Not he only that committeth, but he also that omitteth something, is oftentimes unjust.

V. If my present apprehension of the object be right, and my present action charitable, and this, towards whatsoever doth proceed from God, be my present disposition, to be well pleased with it, it sufficeth.

VI. To wipe away fancy, to use deliberation, to quench concupiscence, to keep the mind free to herself.

VII. Of all unreasonable creatures, there is but one unreasonable soul; and of all that are reasonable, but one reasonable soul, divided betwixt them all. As of all earthly things there is but one earth, and but one light that we see by; and but one air that we breathe in, as many as either breathe or see. Now whatsoever partakes of some common thing, naturally affects and inclines unto that whereof it is part, being of one kind and nature with it. Whatsoever is earthly, presseth downwards to the common earth. Whatsoever is liquid, would flow together. And whatsoever is airy, would be together likewise. So that without some obstacle, and some kind of violence, they cannot well be kept asunder. Whatsoever is fiery, doth not only by reason of the elementary fire tend upwards; but here also is so ready to join, and to burn together, that whatsoever doth want sufficient moisture to make resistance, is easily set on fire. Whatsoever therefore is partaker of that reasonable common nature, naturally doth as much and more long after his own kind. For by how much in its own nature it excels all other things, by so much more is it desirous to be joined and united unto that, which is of its own nature. As for unreasonable creatures then, they had not long been, but presently begun among them swarms, and flocks, and broods of young ones, and a kind of mutual love and affection. For though but unreasonable, yet a kind of soul these had, and therefore was that natural desire of union more strong and intense in them, as in creatures of a more excellent nature, than either in plants, or stones, or trees. But among reasonable creatures, begun commonwealths, friendships, families, public meetings, and even in their wars, conventions, and truces. Now among them that were yet of a more excellent nature, as the stars and planets, though by their nature far distant one from another, yet even among them began some mutual correspondency and unity. So proper is it to excellency in a high degree to affect unity, as that even in things so far distant, it could operate unto a mutual sympathy. But now behold, what is now come to pass. Those creatures that are reasonable, are now the only creatures that have forgotten their natural affection and inclination of one towards another. Among them alone of all other things that are of one kind, there is not to be found a general disposition to flow together. But though they fly from nature, yet are they stopt in their course, and apprehended. Do they what they can, nature doth prevail. And so shalt thou confess, if thou dost observe it. For sooner mayst thou find a thing earthly, where no earthly thing is, than find a man that naturally can live by himself alone.

VIII. Man, God, the world, every one in their kind, bear some fruits. All things have their proper time to bear. Though by custom, the word itself is in a manner become proper unto the vine, and the like, yet is it so nevertheless, as we have said. As for reason, that beareth both common fruit for the use of others; and peculiar, which itself doth enjoy. Reason is of a diffusive nature, what itself is in itself, it begets in others, and so doth multiply.

IX. Either teach them better if it be in thy power; or if it be not, remember that for this use, to bear with them patiently, was mildness and goodness granted unto thee. The Gods themselves are good unto such; yea and in some things, (as in matter of health, of wealth, of honour,) are content often to further their endeavours: so good and gracious are they. And mightest thou not be so too? or, tell me, what doth hinder thee?

X. Labour not as one to whom it is appointed to be wretched, nor as one that either would be pitied, or admired; but let this be thine only care and desire; so always and in all things to prosecute or to forbear, as the law of charity, or mutual society doth require.

XI. This day I did come out of all my trouble. Nay I have cast out all my trouble; it should rather be for that which troubled thee, whatsoever it was, was not without anywhere that thou shouldest come out of it, but within in

Meditations

thine own opinions, from whence it must be cast out, before thou canst truly and constantly be at ease.

XII. All those things, for matter of experience are usual and ordinary; for their continuance but for a day; and for their matter, most base and filthy. As they were in the days of those whom we have buried, so are they now also, and no otherwise.

XIII. The things themselves that affect us, they stand without doors, neither knowing anything themselves nor able to utter anything unto others concerning themselves. What then is it, that passeth verdict on them? The understanding.

XIV. As virtue and wickedness consist not in passion, but in action; so neither doth the true good or evil of a reasonable charitable man consist in passion, but in operation and action.

XV. To the stone that is cast up, when it comes down it is no hurt unto it; as neither benefit, when it doth ascend.

XVI. Sift their minds and understandings, and behold what men they be, whom thou dost stand in fear of what they shall judge of thee, what they themselves judge of themselves.

XVII. All things that are in the world, are always in the estate of alteration. Thou also art in a perpetual change, yea and under corruption too, in some part: and so is the whole world.

XVIII. it is not thine, but another man's sin. Why should it trouble thee? Let him look to it, whose sin it is.

XIX. Of an operation and of a purpose there is an ending, or of an action and of a purpose we say commonly, that it is at an end: from opinion also there is an absolute cessation, which is as it were the death of it. In all this there is no hurt. Apply this now to a man's age, as first, a child; then a youth, then a young man, then an old man; every change from one age to another is a kind of death And all this while here no matter of grief yet. Pass now unto that life first, that which thou livedst under thy grandfather, then under thy mother, then under thy father. And thus when through the whole course of thy life hitherto thou hast found and observed many alterations, many changes, many kinds of endings and cessations, put this question to thyself What matter of grief or sorrow dost thou find in any of these? Or what doest thou suffer through any of these? If in none of these, then neither in the ending and consummation of thy whole life, which is also but a cessation and change.

XX. As occasion shall require, either to thine own understanding, or to that of the universe, or to his, whom thou hast now to do with, let thy refuge be with all speed. To thine own, that it resolve upon nothing against justice. To that of the universe, that thou mayest remember, part of whom thou art. Of his, that thou mayest consider whether in the estate of ignorance, or of knowledge. And then also must thou call to mind, that he is thy kinsman.

XXI. As thou thyself, whoever thou art, were made for the perfection and consummation, being a member of it, of a common society; so must every action of thine tend to the perfection and consummation of a life that is truly sociable. What action soever of thine therefore that either immediately or afar off, hath not reference to the common good, that is an exorbitant and disorderly action;

yea it is seditious; as one among the people who from such and such a consent and unity, should factiously divide and separate himself.

XXII. Children's anger, mere babels; wretched souls bearing up dead bodies, that they may not have their fall so soon: even as it is in that common dirge song.

XXIII. Go to the quality of the cause from which the effect doth proceed. Behold it by itself bare and naked, separated from all that is material. Then consider the utmost bounds of time that that cause, thus and thus qualified, can subsist and abide.

XXIV. Infinite are the troubles and miseries, that thou hast already been put to, by reason of this only, because that for all happiness it did not suffice thee, or, that thou didst not account it sufficient happiness, that thy understanding did operate according to its natural constitution.

XXV. When any shall either impeach thee with false accusations, or hatefully reproach thee, or shall use any such carriage towards thee, get thee presently to their minds and understandings, and look in them, and behold what manner of men they be. Thou shalt see, that there is no such occasion why it should trouble thee, what such as they are think of thee. Yet must thou love them still, for by nature they are thy friends. And the Gods themselves, in those things that they seek from them as matters of great moment, are well content, all manner of ways, as by dreams and oracles, to help them as well as others.

XXVI. Up and down, from one age to another, go the ordinary things of the world; being still the same. And either of everything in particular before it come to pass, the mind of the universe doth consider with itself and deliberate: and if so, then submit for shame unto the determination of such an excellent understanding: or once for all it did resolve upon all things in general; and since that whatsoever happens, happens by a necessary consequence, and all things indivisibly in a manner and inseparably hold one of another. In sum, either there is a God, and then all is well; or if all things go by chance and fortune, yet mayest thou use thine own providence in those things that concern thee properly; and then art thou well.

XXVII. Within a while the earth shall cover us all, and then she herself shall have her change. And then the course will be, from one period of eternity unto another, and so a perpetual eternity. Now can any man that shall consider with himself in his mind the several rollings or successions of so many changes and alterations, and the swiftness of all these rulings; can he otherwise but contemn in his heart and despise all worldly things? The cause of the universe is as it were a strong torrent, it carrieth all away.

XXVIII. And these your professed politicians, the only true practical philosophers of the world, (as they think of themselves) so full of affected gravity, or such professed lovers of virtue and honesty, what wretches be they in very deed; how vile and contemptible in themselves? O man! what ado doest thou keep? Do what thy nature doth now require. Resolve upon it, if thou mayest: and take no thought, whether anybody shall know it or no. Yea, but sayest thou, I must not expect a Plato's commonwealth. If they profit though never so little, I must be content; and think much even of that little progress. Doth then any of them forsake their former false opinions that I should think they profit? For without a change of opinions, alas! what is all that ostentation, but mere wretchedness of slavish minds, that groan privately, and yet would make a show of obedience to reason, and truth? Go too now and tell me of Alexander and Philippus, and Demetrius Phalereus. Whether they understood what the common nature requireth, and could rule themselves or no, they know best themselves. But if they kept a life, and swaggered; I (God be thanked) am not bound to imitate them. The effect of true philosophy is, unaffected simplicity and modesty. Persuade me not to ostentation and vainglory.

XXIX. From some high place as it were to look down, and to behold here flocks, and there sacrifices, without number; and all kind of navigation; some in a rough and stormy sea, and some in a calm: the general differences, or different estates of things, some, that are now first upon being; the several and mutual relations of those things that are together; and some other things that are at their last. Their lives also, who were long ago, and theirs who shall be hereafter, and the present estate and life of those many nations of barbarians that are now in the world, thou must likewise consider in thy mind. And how many there be, who never so much as heard of thy name, how many that will soon forget it; how many who but even now did commend thee, within a very little while perchance will speak ill of thee. So that neither fame, nor honour, nor anything else that this world doth afford, is worth the while. The sum then of all; whatsoever doth happen unto thee, whereof God is the cause, to accept it contentedly: whatsoever thou doest, whereof thou thyself art the cause, to do it justly: which will be, if both in thy resolution and in thy action thou have no further end, than to do good unto others, as being that, which by thy natural constitution, as a man, thou art bound unto.

XXX. Many of those things that trouble and straiten thee, it is in thy power to cut off, as wholly depending from mere conceit and opinion; and then thou shalt have room enough.

XXXI. To comprehend the whole world together in thy mind, and the whole course of this present age to represent it unto thyself, and to fix thy thoughts upon the sudden change of every particular object. How short the time is from the generation of anything, unto the dissolution of the same; but how immense and infinite both that which was before the generation, and that which after the generation of it shall be. All things that thou seest, will soon be perished, and they that see their corruptions, will soon vanish away themselves. He that dieth a hundred years old, and he that dieth young, shall come all to one.

XXXII. What are their minds and understandings; and what the things that they apply themselves unto: what do they love, and what do they hate for? Fancy to thyself the estate of their souls openly to be seen. When they think they hurt them shrewdly, whom they speak ill of; and when they think they do them a very good turn, whom they commend and extol: O how full are they then of conceit, and opinion!

XXXIII. Loss and corruption, is in very deed nothing else but change and alteration; and that is it, which the nature of the universe doth most delight in, by which, and according to which, whatsoever is done, is well done. For that was the estate of worldly things from the beginning, and so shall it ever be. Or wouldest thou rather say, that all things in the world have gone ill from the beginning for so many ages, and shall ever go ill? And then among so many deities, could no divine power be found all this while, that could rectify the things of the world? Or is the world, to incessant woes and miseries, for ever condemned?

XXXIV. How base and putrid, every common matter is! Water, dust, and from the mixture of these bones, and all that loathsome stuff that our bodies do consist of: so subject to be infected, and corrupted. And again those other things that are so much prized and admired, as marble stones, what are they, but as it were the kernels of the earth? gold and silver, what are they, but as the more gross faeces of the earth? Thy most royal apparel, for matter, it is but as it were the hair of a silly sheep, and for colour, the very blood of a shell-fish; of this nature are all other things. Thy life itself, is some such thing too; a mere exhalation of blood: and it also, apt to be changed into some other common thing.

XXXV. Will this querulousness, this murmuring, this complaining and dissembling never be at an end? What then is it, that troubleth thee? Doth any new thing happen unto thee? What doest thou so wonder at? At the cause, or the matter? Behold either by itself, is either of that weight and moment indeed? And besides these, there is not anything. But thy duty towards the Gods also, it is time thou shouldst acquit thyself of it with more goodness and simplicity.

XXXVI. It is all one to see these things for a hundred of years together or but for three years.

XXXVII. If he have sinned, his is the harm, not mine. But perchance he hath not.

XXXVIII. Either all things by the providence of reason happen unto every particular, as a part of one general body; and then it is against reason that a part should complain of anything that happens for the good of the whole; or if, according to Epicurus, atoms be the cause of all things and that life be nothing else but an accidentary confusion of things, and death nothing else, but a mere dispersion and so of all other things: what doest thou trouble thyself for?

XXXIX. Sayest thou unto that rational part, Thou art dead; corruption hath taken hold on thee? Doth it then also void excrements? Doth it like either oxen, or sheep, graze or feed; that it also should be mortal, as well as the body?

XL. Either the Gods can do nothing for us at all, or they can still and allay all the distractions and distempers of thy mind. If they can do nothing, why doest thou pray? If they can, why wouldst not thou rather pray, that they will grant unto thee, that thou mayst neither fear, nor lust after any of those worldly things which cause these distractions and distempers of it? Why not rather, that thou mayst not at either their absence or presence, be grieved and discontented: than either that thou mayst obtain them, or that thou mayst avoid them? For certainly it must needs be, that if the Gods can help us in anything, they may in this kind also. But thou wilt say perchance, 'In those things the Gods have given me my liberty: and it is in mine own power to do what I will.' But if thou mayst use this liberty, rather to set thy mind at true liberty, than wilfully with baseness and servility of mind to affect those things, which either to compass or to avoid is not in thy power, wert not thou better? And as for the Gods, who hath told thee, that they may not help us up even in those things that they have put in our own power? whether it be so or no, thou shalt soon perceive, if thou wilt but try thyself and pray. One prayeth that he may compass his desire, to lie with such or such a one, pray thou that thou mayst not lust to lie with her. Another how he may be rid of such a one; pray thou that thou mayst so patiently bear with him, as that thou have no such need to be rid of him. Another, that he may not lose his child. Pray thou that thou mayst not fear to lose him. To this end and purpose, let all thy prayer be, and see what will be the event.

XLI. 'In my sickness' (saith Epicurus of himself:) 'my discourses were not concerning the nature of my disease, neither was that, to them that came to visit me, the subject of my talk; but in the consideration and contemplation of that, which was of especial weight and moment, was all my time bestowed and spent, and among others in this very thing, how my mind, by a natural and unavoidable sympathy partaking in some sort with the present indisposition of my body, might nevertheless keep herself free from trouble, and in present possession of her own proper happiness. Neither did I leave the ordering of my body to the physicians altogether to do with me what they would, as though I expected any great matter from them, or as though I thought it a matter of such great consequence, by their means to recover my health: for my present estate, methought, liked me very well, and gave me good content.' Whether therefore in sickness (if thou chance to sicken) or in what other kind of extremity soever, endeavour thou also to be in thy mind so affected, as he doth report of himself: not to depart from thy philosophy for anything that can befall thee, nor to give ear to the discourses of silly people, and mere naturalists.

XLII. It is common to all trades and professions to mind and intend that only, which now they are about, and the instrument whereby they work.

XLIII. When at any time thou art offended with any one's impudency, put presently this question to thyself: 'What? Is it then possible, that there should not be any impudent men in the world! Certainly it is not possible.' Desire not then that which is impossible. For this one, (thou must think) whosoever he be, is one of those impudent ones, that the world cannot be without. So of the subtile and crafty, so of the perfidious, so of every one that offendeth, must thou ever be ready to reason with thyself. For whilst in general thou dost thus reason with thyself, that the kind of them must needs be in the world, thou wilt be the better able to use meekness towards every particular. This also thou shalt find of very good use, upon every such occasion, presently to consider with thyself, what proper virtue nature hath furnished man with, against such a vice, or to encounter with a disposition vicious in this kind. As for example, against the unthankful, it hath given goodness and meekness, as an antidote, and so against another vicious in another kind some other peculiar faculty. And generally, is it not in thy power to instruct him better, that is in an error? For whosoever sinneth, doth in that decline from his purposed end, and is certainly deceived, And again, what art thou the worse for his sin? For thou shalt not find that any one of these, against whom thou art incensed, hath in very deed done anything whereby thy mind (the only true subject of thy hurt and evil) can be made worse than it was. And what a matter of either grief or wonder is this, if he that is unlearned, do the deeds of one that is unlearned? Should not thou rather blame thyself, who, when upon very good grounds of reason, thou mightst have thought it very probable, that such a thing would by such a one be committed, didst not only not foresee it, but moreover dost wonder at it, that such a thing should be. But then especially, when thou dost find fault with either an unthankful, or a false man, must thou reflect upon thyself. For without all question, thou thyself art much in fault, if either of one that were of such a disposition, thou didst expect that he should be true unto thee: or when unto any thou didst a good turn, thou didst not there bound thy thoughts, as one that had obtained his end; nor didst not think that from the action itself thou hadst received a full reward of the good that thou hadst done. For what wouldst thou have more? Unto him that is a man, thou hast done a good turn: doth not that suffice thee? What thy nature required, that hast thou done. Must thou be rewarded for it? As if either the eye for that it seeth, or the feet that they go, should require satisfaction. For as these being by nature appointed for such an use, can challenge no more, than that they may work according to their natural constitution: so man being born to do good unto others whensoever he doth a real good unto any by helping them out of error; or though but in middle things, as in matter of wealth, life, preferment, and the like, doth help to further their desires he doth that for which he was made, and therefore can require no more.

THE TENTH BOOK

I. O my soul, the time I trust will be, when thou shalt be good, simple, single, more open and visible, than that body by which it is enclosed. Thou wilt one day be sensible of their happiness, whose end is love, and their affections dead to all worldly things. Thou shalt one day be full, and in want of no external thing: not seeking pleasure from anything, either living or insensible, that this world can afford; neither wanting time for the continuation of thy pleasure, nor place and opportunity, nor the favour either of the weather or of men. When thou shalt have content in thy present estate, and all things present shall add to thy content: when thou shalt persuade thyself, that thou hast all things; all for thy good, and all by the providence of the Gods: and of things future also shalt be as confident, that all will do well, as tending to the maintenance and preservation in some sort, of his perfect welfare and happiness, who is perfection of life, of goodness, and beauty; who begets all things, and containeth all things in himself, and in himself doth recollect all things from all places that are dissolved, that of them he may beget others again like unto them. Such one day shall be thy disposition, that thou shalt be able, both in regard of the Gods, and in regard of men, so to fit and order thy conversation, as neither to complain of them at any time, for anything that they do; nor to do anything thyself, for which thou mayest justly be condemned.

II. As one who is altogether governed by nature, let it be thy care to observe what it is that thy nature in general doth require. That done, if thou find not that thy nature, as thou art a living sensible creature, will be the worse for it, thou mayest proceed. Next then thou must examine, what thy nature as thou art a living sensible creature, doth require. And that, whatsoever it be, thou mayest admit of and do it, if thy nature as thou art a reasonable living creature, will not be the worse for it. Now whatsoever is reasonable, is also sociable, Keep thyself to these rules, and trouble not thyself about idle things.

III. Whatsoever doth happen unto thee, thou art naturally by thy natural constitution either able, or not able to bear. If thou beest able, be not offended, but bear it according to thy natural constitution, or as nature hath enabled thee. If thou beest not able, be not offended. For it will soon make an end of thee, and itself, (whatsoever it be) at the same time end with thee. But remember, that whatsoever by the strength of opinion, grounded upon a certain apprehension of both true profit and duty, thou canst conceive tolerable; that thou art able to bear that by thy natural constitution.

IV. Him that offends, to teach with love and meekness, and to show him his error. But if thou canst not, then to blame thyself; or rather not thyself neither, if thy will and endeavours have not been wanting.

V. Whatsoever it be that happens unto thee, it is that which from all time was appointed unto thee. For by the same coherence of causes, by which thy substance from all eternity was appointed to be, was also whatsoever should happen unto it, destinated and appointed.

VI. Either with Epicurus, we must fondly imagine the atoms to be the cause of all things, or we must needs grant a nature. Let this then be thy first ground, that thou art part of that universe, which is governed by nature. Then secondly, that to those parts that are of the same kind and nature as thou art, thou hast relation of kindred. For of these, if I shall always be mindful, first as I am a part, I shall never be displeased with anything, that falls to my particular share of the common chances of the world. For nothing that is behoveful unto the whole, can be truly hurtful to that which is part of it. For this being the common privilege of all natures, that they contain nothing in themselves that is hurtful unto them; it cannot be that the nature of the universe (whose privilege beyond other particular natures, is, that she cannot against her will by any higher external cause be constrained,) should beget anything and cherish it in her bosom that should tend to her own hurt and prejudice. As then I bear in mind that I am a part of such an universe, I shall not be displeased with anything that happens. And as I have relation of kindred to those parts that are of the same kind and nature that I am, so I shall be careful to do nothing that is prejudicial to the community, but in all my deliberations shall they that are of my kind ever be; and the common good, that, which all my intentions and resolutions shall drive unto, as that which is contrary unto it, I shall by all means endeavour to prevent and avoid. These things once so fixed and concluded, as thou wouldst think him a happy citizen, whose constant study and practice were for the good and benefit of his fellow citizens, and the carriage of the city such towards him, that he were well pleased with it; so must it needs be with thee, that thou shalt live a happy life.

VII. All parts of the world, (all things I mean that are contained within the whole world), must of necessity at some time or other come to corruption. Alteration I should say, to speak truly and properly; but that I may be the better understood, I am content at this time to use that more common word. Now say I, if so be that this be both hurtful unto them, and yet unavoidable, would not, thinkest thou, the whole itself be in a sweet case, all the parts of it being subject to alteration, yea and by their making itself fitted for corruption, as consisting of things different and contrary? And did nature then either of herself thus project and purpose the affliction and misery of her parts, and therefore of purpose so made them, not only that haply they might, but of necessity that they should fall into evil; or did not she know what she did, when she made them? For either of these two to say, is equally absurd. But to let pass nature in general, and to reason of things particular according to their own particular natures; how absurd and ridiculous is it, first to say that all parts of the whole are, by their proper natural constitution, subject to alteration; and then when any such thing doth happen, as when one doth fall sick and dieth, to take on and wonder as though some strange thing had happened? Though this besides might move not so grievously to take on when any such thing doth happen, that whatsoever is dissolved, it is dissolved into those things, whereof it was compounded. For every dissolution is either a mere dispersion, of the elements into those elements again whereof everything did consist, or a change, of that which is more solid into earth; and of that which is pure and subtile or spiritual, into air. So that by this means nothing is lost, but all resumed again into those rational generative seeds of the universe; and this universe, either after a certain period of time to lie consumed by fire, or by continual changes to be renewed, and so for ever to endure. Now that solid and spiritual that we speak of, thou must not conceive it to be that very same, which at first was, when thou wert born. For alas! all this that now thou art in either kind, either for matter of substance, or of life, hath but two or three days ago partly from meats eaten, and partly from air breathed in, received all its influx, being the same then in no other respect, than a running river, maintained by the perpetual influx and new supply of waters, is the same. That therefore which thou hast since received, not that which came from thy mother, is that which comes to change and corruption. But suppose that that for the general substance, and more solid part of it, should still cleave unto thee never so close, yet what is that to the proper qualities and affections of it, by which persons are distinguished, which certainly are quite different?

VIII. Now that thou hast taken these names upon thee of good, modest, true; of ἔμφρων, σύμφρων, ὑπέρφρων; take heed lest at any times by doing anything that is contrary, thou be but improperly so called, and lose thy right to these appellations. Or if thou do, return unto them again with all possible speed. And remember, that the word ἔμφρων notes unto thee an intent and intelligent consideration of every object that presents itself unto thee, without distraction. And the word σύμφρων, a ready and contented acceptation of whatsoever by the appointment of the common nature, happens unto thee. And the word ὑπέρφρων, a super-extension, or a transcendent, and outreaching disposition of thy mind, whereby it passeth by all bodily pains and pleasures, honour and credit, death and whatsoever is of the same nature, as matters of absolute indifferency, and in no wise to be stood upon by a wise man. These then if inviolably thou shalt observe, and shalt not be ambitious to be so called by others, both thou thyself shalt become a new man, and thou shalt begin a new life. For to continue such as hitherto thou hast been, to undergo those distractions and distempers as thou must needs for such a life as hitherto thou hast lived, is the part of one that is very foolish, and is overfond of his life. Whom a man might compare to one of those half-eaten wretches, matched in the amphitheatre with wild beasts; who as full as they are all the body over with wounds and blood, desire for a great favour, that they may be reserved till the next day, then also, and in the same estate to be exposed to the same nails and teeth as before. Away therefore, ship thyself; and from the troubles and distractions of thy former life convey thyself as it were unto these few names; and if thou canst abide in them, or be constant in the practice and possession of them, continue there as glad and joyful as one that were translated unto some such place of bliss and happiness as that which by Hesiod and Plato is called the Islands of the Blessed, by others called the Elysian Fields. And whensoever thou findest thyself; that thou art in danger of a relapse, and that thou art not able to master and overcome those difficulties and temptations that present themselves in thy present station: get thee into any private corner, where thou mayst be better able. Or if that will not serve forsake even thy life rather. But so that it be not in passion but in a plain voluntary modest way: this being the only commendable action of thy whole life that thus thou art departed, or this having been the main work and business of thy whole life, that thou mightest thus depart. Now for the better remembrance of those names that we have spoken of, thou shalt find it a very good help, to remember the Gods as often as may be: and that, the thing which they require at our hands of as many of us, as are by nature reasonable creation is not that with fair words, and outward show of piety and devotion we should flatter them, but that we should become like unto them: and that as all other natural creatures, the fig tree for example; the dog the bee: both do, all of them, and apply themselves unto that which by their natural constitution, is proper unto them; so man likewise should do that, which by his nature, as he is a man, belongs unto him.

IX. Toys and fooleries at home, wars abroad: sometimes terror, sometimes torpor, or stupid sloth: this is thy daily slavery. By little and little, if thou doest not better look to it, those sacred dogmata will be blotted out of thy mind. How many things be there, which when as a mere naturalist, thou hast barely considered of according to their nature, thou doest let pass without any further use? Whereas thou shouldst in all things so join action and contemplation, that thou mightest both at the same time attend all present occasions, to perform everything duly and carefully and yet so intend the contemplative part too, that no part of that delight and pleasure, which the contemplative knowledge of everything according to its true nature doth of itself afford, might be lost. Or, that the true and contemnplative knowledge of everything according to its own nature, might of itself, (action being subject to many lets and impediments) afford unto thee sufficient pleasure and happiness. Not apparent indeed, but not concealed. And when shalt thou attain to the happiness of true simplicity, and unaffected gravity? When shalt thou rejoice in the certain knowledge of every particular object according to its true nature: as what the matter and substance of it is; what use it is for in the world: how long it can subsist: what things it doth consist of: who they be that are capable of it, and who they that can give it, and take it away?

X. As the spider, when it hath caught the fly that it hunted after, is not little proud, nor meanly conceited of herself: as he likewise that hath caught an hare, or hath taken a fish with his net: as another for the taking of a boar, and another of a bear: so may they be proud, and applaud themselves for their valiant acts against the Sarmatai, or northern nations lately defeated. For these also, these famous soldiers and warlike men, if thou dost look into their minds and opinions, what do they for the most part but hunt after prey?

XI. To find out, and set to thyself some certain way and method of contemplation, whereby thou mayest clearly discern and represent unto thyself, the mutual change of all things, the one into the other. Bear it in thy mind evermore, and see that thou be throughly well exercised in this particular. For there is not anything more effectual to beget true magnanimity.

XII. He hath got loose from the bonds of his body, and perceiving that within a very little while he must of necessity bid the world farewell, and leave all these things behind him, he wholly applied himself, as to righteousness in all his actions, so to the common nature in all things that should happen unto him. And contenting himself with these two things, to do all things justly, and whatsoever God doth send to like well of it: what others shall either say or think of him, or shall do against him, he doth not so much as trouble his thoughts with it. To go on straight, whither right and reason directed him, and by so doing to follow God, was the only thing that he did mind, that, his only business and occupation.

XIII. What use is there of suspicion at all? or, why should thoughts of mistrust, and suspicion concerning that which is future, trouble thy mind at all? What now is to be done, if thou mayest search and inquiry into that, what needs thou care for more? And if thou art well able to perceive it alone, let no man divert thee from it. But if alone thou doest not so well perceive it, suspend thine action, and take advice from the best. And if there be anything else that doth hinder thee, go on with prudence and discretion, according to the present occasion and opportunity, still proposing that unto thyself, which thou doest conceive most right and just. For to hit that aright, and to speed in the prosecution of it, must needs be happiness, since it is that only which we can truly and properly be said to miss of, or miscarry in.

XIV. What is that that is slow, and yet quick? merry, and yet grave? He that in all things doth follow reason for his guide.

XV. In the morning as soon as thou art awaked, when thy judgment, before either thy affections, or external objects have wrought upon it, is yet most free and impartial: put this question to thyself, whether if that which is right and just be done, the doing of it by thyself, or by others when thou art not able thyself; be a thing material or no. For sure it is not. And as for these that keep such a life, and stand so much upon the praises, or dispraises of other men, hast thou forgotten what manner of men they be? that such and such upon their beds, and such at their board: what their ordinary actions are: what they pursue after, and what they fly from: what thefts and rapines they commit, if not with their hands and feet, yet with that more precious part of theirs, their minds: which (would it but admit of them) might enjoy faith, modesty, truth, justice, a good spirit.

XVI. Give what thou wilt, and take away what thou wilt, saith he that is well taught and truly modest, to Him that gives, and takes away. And it is not out of a stout and peremptory resolution, that he saith it, but in mere love, and humble submission.

XVII. So live as indifferent to the world and all worldly objects, as one who liveth by himself alone upon some desert hill. For whether here, or there, if the whole world be but as one town, it matters not much for the place. Let them behold and see a man, that is a man indeed, living according to the true nature of man. If they cannot bear with me, let them kill me. For better were it to die, than so to live as they would have thee.

XVIII. Make it not any longer a matter of dispute or discourse, what are the signs and proprieties of a good man, but really and actually to be such.

XIX. Ever to represent unto thyself; and to set before thee, both the general age and time of the world, and the whole substance of it. And how all things particular in respect of these are for their substance, as one of the least seeds that is: and for their duration, as the turning of the pestle in the mortar once about. Then to fix thy mind upon every particular object of the world, and to conceive it, (as it is indeed,) as already being in the state of dissolution, and of change; tending to some kind of either putrefaction or dispersion; or whatsoever else it is, that is the death as it were of everything in his own kind.

XX. Consider them through all actions and occupations, of their lives: as when they eat, and when they sleep: when they are in the act of necessary exoneration, and when in the act of lust. Again, when they either are in their greatest exultation; and in the middle of all their pomp and glory; or being angry and displeased, in great state and majesty, as from an higher place, they chide and rebuke. How base and slavish, but a little while ago, they were fain to be, that they might come to this; and within a very little while what will be their estate, when death hath once seized upon them.

XXI. That is best for every one, that the common nature of all doth send unto every one, and then is it best, when she doth send it.

XXII. The earth, saith the poet, doth often long after the rain. So is the glorious sky often as desirous to fall upon the earth, which argues a mutual kind of love between them. And so (say I) doth the world bear a certain affection of love to whatsoever shall come to pass With thine affections shall mine concur, O world. The same (and no other) shall the object of my longing be which is of thine. Now that the world doth love it is true indeed so is it as commonly said, and acknowledged ledged, when, according to the Greek phrase, imitated by the Latins, of things that used to be, we say commonly, that they love to be.

XXIII. Either thou dost Continue in this kind of life and that is it, which so long thou hast been used unto and therefore tolerable: or thou doest retire, or leave the world, and that of thine own accord, and then thou hast thy mind: or thy life is cut off; and then mayst thou rejoice that thou hast ended thy charge. One of these must needs be. Be therefore of good comfort.

Meditations

XXIV Let it always appear and be manifest unto thee that solitariness, and desert places, by many philosophers so much esteemed of and affected, are of themselves but thus and thus; and that all things are them to them that live in towns, and converse with others as they are the same nature everywhere to be seen and observed: to them that have retired themselves to the top of mountains, and to desert havens, or what other desert and inhabited places soever. For anywhere it thou wilt mayest thou quickly find and apply that to thyself; which Plato saith of his philosopher, in a place: as private and retired, saith he, as if he were shut up and enclosed about in some shepherd's lodge, on the top of a hill. There by thyself to put these questions to thyself or to enter in these considerations: What is my chief and principal part, which hath power over the rest? What is now the present estate of it, as I use it; and what is it, that I employ it about? Is it now void of reason ir no? Is it free, and separated; or so affixed, so congealed and grown together as it were with the flesh, that it is swayed by the motions and inclinations of it?

XXV. He that runs away from his master is a fugitive. But the law is every man's master. He therefore that forsakes the law, is a fugitive. So is he, whosoever he be, that is either sorry, angry, or afraid, or for anything that either hath been, is, or shall be by his appointment, who is the Lord and Governor of the universe. For he truly and properly is Νόμος, or the law, as the only νέμων, or distributor and dispenser of all things that happen unto any one in his lifetime—Whatsoever then is either sorry, angry, or afraid, is a fugitive.

XXVI. From man is the seed, that once cast into the womb man hath no more to do with it. Another cause succeedeth, and undertakes the work, and in time brings a child (that wonderful effect from such a beginning!) to perfection. Again, man lets food down through his throat; and that once down, he hath no more to do with it. Another cause succeedeth and distributeth this food into the senses, and the affections: into life, and into strength; and doth with it those other many and marvellous things, that belong unto man. These things therefore that are so secretly and invisibly wrought and brought to pass, thou must use to behold and contemplate; and not the things themselves only, but the power also by which they are effected; that thou mayst behold it, though not with the eyes of the body, yet as plainly and visibly as thou canst see and discern the outward efficient cause of the depression and elevation of anything.

XXVII. Ever to mind and consider with thyself; how all things that now are, have been heretofore much after the same sort, and after the same fashion that now they are: and so to think of those things which shall be hereafter also. Moreover, whole dramata, and uniform scenes, or scenes that comprehend the lives and actions of men of one calling and profession, as many as either in thine own experience thou hast known, or by reading of ancient histories; (as the whole court of Adrianus, the whole court of Antoninus Pius, the whole court of Philippus, that of Alexander, that of Crœsus): to set them all before thine eyes. For thou shalt find that they are all but after one sort and fashion: only that the actors were others.

XXVIII. As a pig that cries and flings when his throat is cut, fancy to thyself every one to be, that grieves for any worldly thing and takes on. Such a one is he also, who upon his bed alone, doth bewail the miseries of this our mortal life. And remember this, that Unto reasonable creatures only it is granted that they may willingly and freely submit unto Providence: but absolutely to submit, is a necessity imposed upon all creatures equally.

XXIX. Whatsoever it is that thou goest about, consider of it by thyself, and ask thyself, What? because I shall do this no more when I am dead, should therefore death seem grievous unto me?

XXX. When thou art offended with any man's transgression, presently reflect upon thyself; and consider what thou thyself art guilty of in the same kind. As that thou also perchance dost think it a happiness either to be rich, or to live in pleasure, or to be praised and commended, and so of the rest in particular. For this if thou shalt call to mind, thou shalt soon forget thine anger; especially when at the same time this also shall concur in thy thoughts, that he was constrained by his error and ignorance so to do: for how can he choose as long as he is of that opinion? Do thou therefore if thou canst, take away that from him, that forceth him to do as he doth.

XXXI. When thou seest Satyro, think of Socraticus and Eutyches, or Hymen, and when Euphrates, think of Eutychio, and Sylvanus, when Alciphron, of Tropaeophorus, when Xenophon, of Crito, or Severus. And when thou doest look upon thyself, fancy unto thyself some one or other of the Cæsars; and so for every one, some one or other that hath been for estate and profession answerable unto him. Then let this come to thy mind at the same time; and where now are they all? Nowhere or anywhere? For so shalt thou at all time be able to perceive how all worldly things are but as the smoke, that vanisheth away: or, indeed, mere nothing. Especially when thou shalt call to mind this also, that whatsoever is once changed, shall never be again as long as the world endureth. And thou then, how long shalt thou endure? And why doth it not suffice thee, if virtuously, and as becometh thee, thou mayest pass that portion of time, how little soever it be, that is allotted unto thee?

XXXII. What a subject, and what a course of life is it, that thou doest so much desire to be rid of. For all these things, what are they, but fit objects for an understanding, that beholdeth everything according to its true nature, to exercise itself upon? Be patient, therefore, until that (as a strong stomach that turns all things into his own nature; and as a great fire that turneth in flame and light, whatsoever thou doest cast into it) thou have made these things also familiar, and as it were natural unto thee.

XXXIII. Let it not be in any man's power, to say truly of thee, that thou art not truly simple, or sincere and open, or not good. Let him be deceived whosoever he be that shall have any such opinion of thee. For all this doth depend of thee. For who is it that should hinder thee from being either truly simple or good? Do thou only resolve rather not to live, than not to be such. For indeed neither doth it stand with reason that he should live that is not such. What then is it that may upon this present occasion according to best reason and discretion, either be said or done? For whatsoever it be, it is in thy power either to do it, or to say it, and therefore seek not any pretences, as though thou wert hindered. Thou wilt never cease groaning and complaining, until such time as that, what pleasure is unto the voluptuous, be unto thee, to do in everything that presents itself, whatsoever may be done conformably and agreeably to the proper constitution of man, or, to man as he is a man. For thou must account that pleasure, whatsoever it be, that thou mayest do according to thine own nature. And to do this, every place will fit thee. Unto the *cylindrus*, or roller, it is not granted to move everywhere according to its own proper motion, as neither unto the water, nor unto the fire, nor unto any other thing, that either is merely natural, or natural and sensitive; but not rational for many things there be that can hinder their operations. But of the mind and understanding this is the proper privilege, that according to its own nature, and as it will itself, it can pass through every obstacle that it finds, and keep straight on forwards. Setting therefore before thine eyes this happiness and felicity of thy mind, whereby it is able to pass through all things, and is capable of all motions, whether as the fire, upwards; or as the stone downwards, or as the *cylindrus* through that which is sloping: content thyself with it, and seek not after any other thing. For all other kind of hindrances that are not hindrances of thy mind either they are proper to the body, or merely proceed from the opinion, reason not making that resistance that it should, but basely, and cowardly suffering itself to be foiled; and of themselves can neither wound, nor do any hurt at all. Else must he of necessity, whosoever he be that meets with any of them, become worse than he was before. For so is it in all other subjects, that that is thought hurtful unto them, whereby they are made worse. But here contrariwise, man (if he make that good use of them that he should) is rather the better and the more praiseworthy for any of those kind of hindrances, than otherwise. But generally remember that nothing can hurt a natural citizen, that is not hurtful unto the city itself, nor anything hurt the city, that is not hurtful unto the law itself. But none of these casualties, or external hindrances, do hurt the law itself; or, are contrary to that course of justice and equity, by which public societies are maintained: neither therefore do they hurt either city or citizen.

XXXIV. As he that is bitten by a mad dog, is afraid of everything almost that he seeth: so unto him, whom the dogmata have once bitten, or in whom true knowledge hath made an impression, everything almost that he sees or reads be it never so short or ordinary, doth afford a good memento; to put him out of all grief and fear, as that of the poet, 'The winds blow upon the trees, and their leaves fall upon the ground. Then do the trees begin to bud again, and by the spring-time they put forth new branches. So is the generation of men; some come into the world, and others go out of it.' Of these leaves then thy children are. And they also that applaud thee so gravely, or, that applaud thy speeches, with that their usual acclamation, ἀξιοπίστως, O wisely spoken I and speak well of thee, as on the other side, they that stick not to curse thee, they that privately and secretly dispraise and deride thee, they also are but leaves. And they also that shall follow, in whose memories the names of men famous after death, is preserved, they are but leaves neither. For even so is it of all these worldly things. Their spring comes, and they are put forth. Then blows the wind, and they go down. And then in lieu of them grow others out of the wood or common matter of all things, like unto them. But, to endure but for a while, is common unto all. Why then shouldest thou so earnestly either seek after these things, or fly from them, as though they should endure for ever? Yet a little while, and thine eyes will be closed up, and for him that carries thee to thy grave shall another mourn within a while after.

XXXV. A good eye must be good to see whatsoever is to be seen, and not green things only. For that is proper to sore eyes. So must a good ear, and a good smell be ready for whatsoever is either to be heard, or smelt: and a good stomach as indifferent to all kinds of food, as a millstone is, to whatsoever she was made for to grind. As ready therefore must a sound understanding be for whatsoever shall happen. But he that saith, O that my children might live! and, O that all men might commend me for whatsoever I do! is an eye that seeks after green things; or as teeth, after that which is tender.

XXXVI. There is not any man that is so happy in his death, but that some of those that are by him when he dies, will be ready to rejoice at his supposed calamity. Is it one that was virtuous and wise indeed? will there not some one or other be found, who thus will say to himself; 'Well now at last shall I be at rest from this pedagogue. He did not indeed otherwise trouble us much: but I know well enough that in his heart, he did much condemn us.' Thus will they speak of the virtuous. But as for us, alas I how many things be there, for which there be many that glad would be to be rid of us. This therefore if thou shalt think of whensoever thou diest, thou shalt die the more willingly, when thou shalt think with thyself; I am now to depart from that world, wherein those that have been my nearest friends and acquaintances, they whom I have so much suffered for, so often prayed for, and for whom I have taken such care, even they would have me die, hoping that after my death they shall live happier, than they did before. What then should any man desire to continue here any longer? Nevertheless, whensoever thou diest, thou must not be less kind and loving unto them for it; but as before, see them, continue to be their friend, to wish them well, and meekly, and gently to carry thyself towards them, but yet so that on the other side, it make thee not the more unwilling to die. But as it fareth with them that die an easy quick death, whose soul is soon separated from their bodies, so must thy separation from them be. To these had nature joined and annexed me: now she parts us; I am ready to depart, as from friends and kinsmen, but yet without either reluctancy or compulsion. For this also is according to Nature.

XXXVII. Use thyself; as often, as thou seest any man do anything, presently (if it be possible) to say unto thyself, What is this man's end in this his action? But begin this course with thyself first of all, and diligently examine thyself concerning whatsoever thou doest.

XXXVIII. Remember, that that which sets a man at work, and hath power over the affections to draw them either one way, or the other way, is not any external thing properly, but that which is hidden within every man's dogmata, and opinions: That, that is rhetoric; that is life; that (to speak true) is man himself. As for thy body, which as a vessel, or a case, compasseth thee about, and the many and curious instruments that it hath annexed unto it, let them not trouble thy thoughts. For of themselves they are but as a carpenter's axe, but that they are born with us, and naturally sticking unto us. But otherwise, without the inward cause that hath power to move them, and to restrain them, those parts are of themselves of no more use unto us, than the shuttle is of itself to the weaver, or the pen to the writer, or the whip to the coachman.

THE ELEVENTH BOOK

I. The natural properties, and privileges of a reasonable soul are: That she seeth herself; that she can order, and compose herself: that she makes herself as she will herself: that she reaps her own fruits whatsoever, whereas plants, trees, unreasonable creatures, what fruit soever (be it either fruit properly, or analogically only) they bear, they bear them unto others, and not to themselves. Again; whensoever, and wheresoever, sooner or later, her life doth end, she hath her own end nevertheless. For it is not with her, as with dancers and players, who if they be interrupted in any part of their action, the whole action must needs be imperfect: but she in what part of time or action soever she be surprised, can make that which she hath in her hand whatsoever it be, complete and full, so that she may depart with that comfort, 'I have lived; neither want I anything of that which properly did belong unto me.' Again, she compasseth the whole world, and penetrateth into the vanity, and mere outside (wanting substance and solidity) of it, and stretcheth herself unto the infiniteness of eternity; and the revolution or restoration of all things after a certain period of time, to the same state and place as before, she fetcheth about, and doth comprehend in herself; and considers withal, and sees clearly this, that neither they that shall follow us, shall see any new thing, that we have not seen, nor they that went before, anything more than we: but that he that is once come to forty (if he have any wit at all) can in a manner (for that they are all of one kind) see all things, both past and future. As proper is it, and natural to the soul of man to love her neighbour, to be true and modest; and to regard nothing so much as herself: which is also the property of the law: whereby by the way it appears, that sound reason and justice comes all to one, and therefore that justice is the chief thing, that reasonable creatures ought to propose unto themselves as their end.

II. A pleasant song or dance; the Pancratiast's exercise, sports that thou art wont to be much taken with, thou shalt easily contemn; if the harmonious voice thou shalt divide into so many particular sounds whereof it doth consist, and of every one in particular shall ask thyself; whether this or that sound is it, that doth so conquer thee. For thou wilt be ashamed of it. And so for shame, if accordingly thou shalt consider it, every particular motion and posture by itself: and so for the wrestler's exercise too. Generally then, whatsoever it be, besides virtue, and those things that proceed from virtue that thou art subject to be much affected with, remember presently thus to divide it, and by this kind of division, in each particular to attain unto the contempt of the whole. This thou must transfer and apply to thy whole life also.

III. That soul which is ever ready, even now presently (if need be) from the body, whether by way of extinction, or dispersion, or continuation in another place and estate to be separated, how blessed and happy is it! But this readiness of it, it must proceed, not from an obstinate and peremptory resolution of the mind, violently and passionately set upon Opposition, as Christians are wont;

but from a peculiar judgment; with discretion and gravity, so that others may be persuaded also and drawn to the like example, but without any noise and passionate exclamations.

IV. Have I done anything charitably? then am I benefited by it. See that this upon all occasions may present itself unto thy mind, and never cease to think of it. What is thy profession? to be good. And how should this be well brought to pass, but by certain theorems and doctrines; some Concerning the nature of the universe, and some Concerning the proper and particular constitution of man?

V. Tragedies were at first brought in and instituted, to put men in mind of worldly chances and casualties: that these things in the ordinary course of nature did so happen: that men that were much pleased and delighted by such accidents upon this stage, would not by the same things in a greater stage be grieved and afflicted: for here you see what is the end of all such things; and that even they that cry out so mournfully to Cithaeron, must bear them for all their cries and exclamations, as well as others. And in very truth many good things are spoken by these poets; as that (for example) is an excellent passage: 'But if so be that I and my two children be neglected by the Gods, they have some reason even for that,' &c. And again, 'It will but little avail thee to storm and rage against the things themselves,' &c. Again, 'To reap one's life, as a ripe ear of corn;' and whatsoever else is to be found in them, that is of the same kind. After the tragedy, the ancient comedy was brought in, which had the liberty to inveigh against personal vices; being therefore through this her freedom and liberty of speech of very good use and effect, to restrain men from pride and arrogancy. To which end it was, that Diogenes took also the same liberty. After these, what were either the Middle, or New Comedy admitted for, but merely, (Or for the most part at least) for the delight and pleasure of curious and excellent imitation? 'It will steal away; look to it,' &c. Why, no man denies, but that these also have some good things whereof that may be one: but the whole drift and foundation of that kind of dramatical poetry, what is it else, but as we have said?

VI. How clearly doth it appear unto thee, that no other course of thy life could fit a true philosopher's practice better, than this very course, that thou art now already in?

VII. A branch cut off from the continuity of that which was next unto it, must needs be cut off from the whole tree: so a man that is divided from another man, is divided from the whole society. A branch is cut off by another, but he that hates and is averse, cuts himself off from his neighbour, and knows not that at the same time he divides himself from the whole body, or corporation. But herein is the gift and mercy of God, the Author of this society, in that, once cut off we may grow together and become part of the whole again. But if this happen often the misery is that the further a man is run in this division, the harder he is to be reunited and restored again: and however the branch which, once cut of afterwards was graffed in, gardeners can tell you is not like that which sprouted together at first, and still continued in the unity of the body.

VIII. To grow together like fellow branches in matter of good correspondence and affection; but not in matter of opinions. They that shall oppose thee in thy right courses, as it is not in their power to divert thee from thy good action, so neither let it be to divert thee from thy good affection towards them. But be it thy care to keep thyself constant in both; both in a right judgment and action, and in true meekness towards them, that either shall do their endeavour to hinder thee, or at least will be displeased with thee for what thou hast done. For to fail in either (either in the one to give over for fear, or in the other to forsake thy natural affection towards him, who by nature is both thy friend and thy kinsman) is equally base, and much savouring of the disposition of a cowardly fugitive soldier.

IX. It is not possible that any nature should be inferior unto art, since that all arts imitate nature. If this be so; that the most perfect and general nature of all natures should in her operation come short of the skill of arts, is most improbable. Now common is it to all arts, to make that which is worse for the better's sake. Much more then doth the common nature do the same. Hence is the first ground of justice. From justice all other virtues have their existence. For justice cannot be preserved, if either we settle our minds and affections upon worldly things; or be apt to be deceived, or rash, and inconstant.

X. The things themselves (which either to get or to avoid thou art put to so much trouble) come not unto thee themselves; but thou in a manner goest unto them. Let then thine own judgment and opinion concerning those things be at rest; and as for the things themselves, they stand still and quiet, without any noise or stir at all; and so shall all pursuing and flying cease.

XI. Then is the soul as Empedocles doth liken it, like unto a sphere or globe, when she is all of one form and figure: when she neither greedily stretcheth out herself unto anything, nor basely contracts herself, or lies flat and dejected; but shineth all with light, whereby she does see and behold the true nature, both that of the universe, and her own in particular.

XII. Will any contemn me? let him look to that, upon what grounds he does it: my care shall be that I may never be found either doing or speaking anything that doth truly deserve contempt. Will any hate me? let him look to that. I for my part will be kind and loving unto all, and even unto him that hates me, whom-soever he be, will I be ready to show his error, not by way of exprobation or ostentation of my patience, but ingenuously and meekly: such as was that famous Phocion, if so be that he did not dissemble. For it is inwardly that these things must be: that the Gods who look inwardly, and not upon the outward appearance, may behold a man truly free from all indignation and grief. For what hurt can it be unto thee whatsoever any man else doth, as long as thou mayest do that which is proper and suitable to thine own nature? Wilt not thou (a man wholly appointed to be both what, and as the common good shall require) accept of that which is now seasonable to the nature of the universe?

XIII. They contemn one another, and yet they seek to please one another: and whilest they seek to surpass one another in worldly pomp and greatness, they most debase and prostitute themselves in their better part one to another.

XIV. How rotten and insincere is he, that saith, I am resolved to carry myself hereafter towards you with all ingenuity and simplicity. O man, what doest thou mean! what needs this profession of thine? the thing itself will show it. It ought to be written upon thy forehead. No sooner thy voice is heard, than thy countenance must be able to show what is in thy mind: even as he that is loved knows presently by the looks of his sweetheart what is in her mind. Such must he be for all the world, that is truly simple and good, as he whose arm-holes are offensive, that whosoever stands by, as soon as ever he comes near him, may as it were smell him whether he will or no. But the affectation of simplicity is nowise laudable. There is nothing more shameful than perfidious friendship. Above all things, that must be avoided. However true goodness, simplicity, and kindness cannot so be hidden, but that as we have already said in the very eyes and countenance they will show themselves.

XV. To live happily is an inward power of the soul, when she is affected with indifferency, towards those things that are by their nature indifferent. To be thus affected she must consider all worldly objects both divided and whole: remembering withal that no object can of itself beget any opinion in us, neither can come to us, but stands without still and quiet; but that we ourselves beget, and as it were print in ourselves opinions concerning them. Now it is in our power, not to print them; and if they creep in and lurk in some corner, it is in our power to wipe them off. Remembering moreover, that this care and circumspection of thine, is to continue but for a while, and then thy life will be at an end. And what should hinder, but that thou mayest do well with all these things? For if they be according to nature, rejoice in them, and let them be pleasing and acceptable unto thee. But if they be against nature, seek thou that which is according to thine own nature, and whether it be for thy credit or no, use all possible speed for the attainment of it: for no man ought to be blamed, for seeking his own good and happiness.

XVI. Of everything thou must consider from whence it came, of what things it doth consist, and into what it will be changed: what will be the nature of it, or what it will be like unto when it is changed; and that it can suffer no hurt by this change. And as for other men's either foolishness or wickedness, that it may not trouble and grieve thee; first generally thus; What reference have I unto these? and that we are all born for one another's good: then more particularly after another consideration; as a ram is first in a flock of sheep, and a bull in a herd of cattle, so am I born to rule over them. Begin yet higher, even from this: if atoms be not the beginning of all things, than which to believe nothing can be more absurd, then must we needs grant that there is a nature, that doth govern the universe. If such a nature, then are all worse things made for the better's sake; and all better for one another's sake. Secondly, what manner of men they be, at board, and upon their beds, and so forth. But above all things, how they are forced by their opinions that they hold, to do what they do; and even those things that they do, with what pride and self-conceit they do them. Thirdly, that if they do these things rightly, thou hast no reason to be grieved. But if not rightly, it must needs be that they do them against their wills, and through mere ignorance. For as, according to Plato's opinion, no soul doth willingly err, so by consequent neither doth it anything otherwise than it ought, but against her will. Therefore are they grieved, whensoever they hear themselves charged, either of injustice, or unconscionableness, or covetousness, or in general, of any injurious kind of dealing towards their neighbours. Fourthly, that thou thyself doest transgress in many things, and art even such another as they are. And though perchance thou doest forbear the very act of some sins, yet hast thou in thyself an habitual disposition to them, but that either through fear, or vainglory, or some such other ambitious foolish respect, thou art restrained. Fifthly, that whether they have sinned or no, thou doest not understand perfectly. For many things are done by way of discreet policy; and generally a man must know many things first, before he be able truly and judiciously to judge of another man's action. Sixthly, that whensoever thou doest take on grievously, or makest great woe, little doest thou remember then that a man's life is but for a moment of time, and that within a while we shall all be in our graves. Seventhly, that it is not the sins and transgressions themselves that trouble us properly; for they have their existence in their minds and understandings only, that commit them; but our own opinions concerning those sins. Remove then, and be content to part with that conceit of thine, that it is a grievous thing, and thou hast removed thine anger. But how should I remove it? How? reasoning with thyself that it is not shameful. For if that which is shameful, be not the only true evil that is, thou also wilt be driven whilest thou doest follow the common instinct of nature, to avoid that which is evil, to commit many unjust things, and to become a thief, and anything, that will make to the attainment of thy intended worldly ends. Eighthly, how many things may and do oftentimes follow upon such fits of anger and grief; far more grievous in themselves, than those very things which we are so grieved or angry for. Ninthly, that meekness is a thing unconquerable, if it be true and natural, and not affected or hypocritical. For how shall even the most fierce and malicious that thou shalt conceive, be able to hold on against thee, if thou shalt still continue meek and loving unto him; and that even at that time, when he is about to do thee wrong, thou shalt be well disposed, and in good temper, with all meekness to teach him, and to instruct him better? As for example; My son, we were not born for this, to hurt and annoy one another; it will be thy hurt not mine, my son: and so to show him forcibly and fully, that it is so in very deed: and that neither bees do it one to another, nor any other creatures that are naturally sociable. But this thou must do, not scoffingly, not by way of exprobation, but tenderly without any harshness of words. Neither must thou do it by way of exercise, or ostentation, that they that are by and hear thee, may admire thee: but so always that nobody be privy to it, but himself alone: yea, though there be more present at the same time. These nine particular heads, as so many gifts from the Muses, see that thou remember well: and begin one day, whilest thou art yet alive, to be a man indeed. But on the other side thou must take heed, as much to flatter them, as to be angry with them: for both are equally uncharitable, and equally hurtful. And in thy passions, take it presently to thy consideration, that to be angry is not the part of a man, but that to be meek and gentle, as it savours of more humanity, so of more manhood. That in this, there is strength and nerves, or vigour and fortitude: whereof anger and indignation is altogether void. For the nearer everything is unto unpassionateness, the nearer it is unto power. And as grief doth proceed from weakness, so doth anger. For both, both he that is angry and that grieveth, have received a wound, and cowardly have as it were yielded themselves unto their affections. If thou wilt have a tenth also, receive this tenth gift from Hercules the guide and leader of the Muses: that is a mad man's part, to look that there should be no wicked men in the world, because it is impossible. Now for a man to brook well enough, that there should be wicked men in the world, but not to endure that any should transgress against himself, is against all equity, and indeed tyrannical.

XVII. Four several dispositions or inclinations there be of the mind and understanding, which to be aware of, thou must carefully observe: and whensoever thou doest discover them, thou must rectify them, saying to thyself concerning every one of them, This imagination is not necessary; this is uncharitable: this thou shalt speak as another man's slave, or instrument; than which nothing can be more senseless and absurd: for the fourth, thou shalt sharply check and upbraid thyself; for that thou doest suffer that more divine part in thee, to become subject and obnoxious to that more ignoble part of thy body, and the gross lusts and concupiscences thereof.

XVIII. What portion soever, either of air or fire there be in thee, although by nature it tend upwards, submitting nevertheless to the ordinance of the universe, it abides here below in this mixed body. So whatsoever is in thee, either earthy, or humid, although by nature it tend downwards, yet is it against its nature both raised upwards, and standing, or consistent. So obedient are even the elements themselves to the universe, abiding patiently wheresoever (though against their nature) they are placed, until the sound as it were of their retreat, and separation. Is it not a grievous thing then, that thy reasonable part only should be disobedient, and should not endure to keep its place: yea though it be nothing enjoined that is contrary unto it, but that only which is according to its nature? For we cannot say of it when it is disobedient, as we say of the fire, or air, that it tends upwards towards its proper element, for then goes it the quite contrary way. For the motion of the mind to any injustice, or incontinency, or to sorrow, or to fear, is nothing else but a separation from nature. Also when the mind is grieved for anything that is happened by the divine providence, then doth it likewise forsake its own place. For it was ordained unto holiness and godliness, which specially consist in an humble submission to God and His providence in all things; as well as unto justice: these also being part of those duties, which as naturally sociable, we are bound unto; and without which we cannot happily converse one with another: yea and the very ground and fountain indeed of all just actions.

XIX. He that hath not one and the self-same general end always as long as he liveth, cannot possibly be one and the self-same man always. But this will not suffice except thou add also what ought to be this general end. For as the general conceit and apprehension of all those things which upon no certain ground are by the greater part of men deemed good, cannot be uniform and agreeable, but that only which is limited and restrained by some certain proprieties and conditions, as of community: that nothing be conceived good, which is not commonly and publicly good: so must the end also that we propose unto ourselves, be common and sociable. For he that doth direct all his own private motions and purposes to that end, all his actions will be agreeable and uniform; and by that means will be still the same man.

XX. Remember the fable of the country mouse and the city mouse, and the great fright and terror that this was put into.

XXI. Socrates was wont to call the common conceits and opinions of men, the common bugbears of the world: the proper terror of silly children.

XXII. The Lacedæmonians at their public spectacles were wont to appoint seats and forms for their strangers in the shadow, they themselves were content to sit anywhere.

XXIII. What Socrates answered unto Perdiccas, why he did not come unto him, Lest of all deaths I should die the worst kind of death, said he: that is, not able to requite the good that hath been done unto me.

XXIV. In the ancient mystical letters of the Ephesians, there was an item, that a man should always have in his mind some one or other of the ancient worthies.

XXV. The Pythagoreans were wont betimes in the morning the first thing they did, to look up unto the heavens, to put themselves in mind of them who constantly and invariably did perform their task: as also to put themselves in mind of orderliness, or good order, and of purity, and of naked simplicity. For no star or planet hath any cover before it.

XXVI. How Socrates looked, when he was fain to gird himself with a skin, Xanthippe his wife having taken away his clothes, and carried them abroad with her, and what he said to his fellows and friends, who were ashamed; and out of respect to him, did retire themselves when they saw him thus decked.

XXVII. In matter of writing or reading thou must needs be taught before thou can do either: much more in matter of life. 'For thou art born a mere slave, to thy senses and brutish affections;' destitute without teaching of all true knowledge and sound reason.

XXVIII. 'My heart smiled within me.' 'They will accuse even virtue herself; with heinous and opprobrious words.'

XXIX. As they that long after figs in winter when they cannot be had; so are they that long after children, before they be granted them.

XXX. 'As often as a father kisseth his child, he should say secretly with himself' (said Epictetus,) 'tomorrow perchance shall he die.' But these words be ominous. No words ominous (said he) that signify anything that is natural: in very truth and deed not more ominous than this, 'to cut down grapes when they are ripe.' Green grapes, ripe grapes, dried grapes, or raisins: so many changes and mutations of one thing, not into that which was not absolutely, but rather so many several changes and mutations, not into that which hath no being at all, but into that which is not yet in being.

XXXI. 'Of the free will there is no thief or robber:' out of Epictetus; Whose is this also: that we should find a certain art and method of assenting; and that we should always observe with great care and heed the inclinations of our minds, that they may always be with their due restraint and reservation, always charitable, and according to the true worth of every present object. And as for earnest longing, that we should altogether avoid it: and to use averseness in those things only, that wholly depend of our own wills. It is not about ordinary petty matters, believe it, that all our strife and contention is, but whether, with the vulgar, we should be mad, or by the help of philosophy wise and sober, said he. XXXII. Socrates said, 'What will you have? the souls of reasonable, or unreasonable creatures? Of reasonable. But what? Of those whose reason is sound and perfect? or of those whose reason is vitiated and corrupted? Of those whose reason is sound and perfect. Why then labour ye not for such? Because we have them already. What then do ye so strive and contend between you?'

THE TWELFTH BOOK

I. Whatsoever thou doest hereafter aspire unto, thou mayest even now enjoy and possess, if thou doest not envy thyself thine own happiness. And that will be, if thou shalt forget all that is past, and for the future, refer thyself wholly to the Divine Providence, and shalt bend and apply all thy present thoughts and intentions to holiness and righteousness. To holiness, in accepting willingly whatsoever is sent by the Divine Providence, as being that which the nature of the universe hath appointed unto thee, which also hath appointed thee for that, whatsoever it be. To righteousness, in speaking the truth freely, and without ambiguity; and in doing all things justly and discreetly. Now in this good course, let not other men's either wickedness, or opinion, or voice hinder thee: no, nor the sense of this thy pampered mass of flesh: for let that which suffers, look to itself. If therefore whensoever the time of thy departing shall come, thou shalt readily leave all things, and shalt respect thy mind only, and that divine part of thine, and this shall be thine only fear, not that some time or other thou shalt cease to live, but thou shalt never begin to live according to nature: then shalt thou be a man indeed, worthy of that world, from which thou hadst thy beginning; then shalt thou cease to be a stranger in thy country, and to wonder at those things that happen daily, as things strange and unexpected, and anxiously to depend of divers things that are not in thy power.

II. God beholds our minds and understandings, bare and naked from these material vessels, and outsides, and all earthly dross. For with His simple and pure understanding, He pierceth into our inmost and purest parts, which from His, as it were by a water pipe and channel, first flowed and issued. This if thou also shalt use to do, thou shalt rid thyself of that manifold luggage, wherewith thou art round about encumbered. For he that does regard neither his body, nor his clothing, nor his dwelling, nor any such external furniture, must needs gain unto himself great rest and ease. Three things there be in all, which thou doest consist of; thy body, thy life, and thy mind. Of these the two former, are so far forth thine, as that thou art bound to take care for them. But the third alone is that which is properly thine. If then thou shalt separate from thyself, that is from thy mind, whatsoever other men either do or say, or whatsoever thou thyself hast heretofore either done or said; and all troublesome thoughts concerning the future, and whatsoever, (as either belonging to thy body or life:) is without the jurisdiction of thine own will, and whatsoever in the ordinary course of human chances and accidents doth happen unto thee; so that thy mind (keeping herself loose and free from all outward coincidental entanglements; always in a readiness to depart:) shall live by herself, and to herself, doing that which is just, accepting whatsoever doth happen, and speaking the truth always; if, I say, thou shalt separate from thy mind, whatsoever by sympathy might adhere unto it, and all time both past and future, and shalt make thyself in all points and respects, like unto Empedocles his allegorical sphere, 'all round and circular,' &c., and shalt think of no longer life than that which is now present: then shalt thou be truly able to pass the remainder of thy days without troubles and distractions; nobly and generously disposed, and in good favour and correspondency, with that spirit which is within thee.

III. I have often wondered how it should come to pass, that every man loving himself best, should more regard other men's opinions concerning himself than his own. For if any God or grave master standing by, should command any of us to think nothing by himself but what he should presently speak out; no man were able to endure it, though but for one day. Thus do we fear more what our neighbours will think of us, than what we ourselves.

IV. how come it to pass that the Gods having ordered all other things so well and so lovingly, should be overseen in this onc only thing, that whereas then hath been some very good men that have made many covenants as it were with God and by many holy actions and outward services contracted a kind of familiarity with Him; that these men when once they are dead, should never be restored to life, but be extinct for ever. But this thou mayest be sure of, that this (if it be so indeed) would never have been so ordered by the Gods, had it been fit otherwise. For certainly it was possible, had it been more just so and had it been according to nature, the nature of the universe would easily have borne it. But now because it is not so, (if so be that it be not so indeed) be therefore confident that it was not fit it should be so for thou seest thyself, that now seeking after this matter, how freely thou doest argue and contest with God. But were not the Gods both just and good in the highest degree, thou durst not thus reason with them. Now if just and good, it could not be that in the creation of the world, they should either unjustly or unreasonably oversee anything.

V. Use thyself even unto those things that thou doest at first despair of. For the left hand we see, which for the most part lieth idle because not used; yet doth it hold the bridle with more strength than the right, because it hath been used unto it.

VI. Let these be the objects of thy ordinary meditation: to consider, what manner of men both for soul and body we ought to be, whensoever death shall surprise us: the shortness of this our mortal life: the immense vastness of the time that hath been before, and will he after us: the frailty of every worldly material object: all these things to consider, and behold clearly in themselves, all disguisement of external outside being removed and taken away. Again, to consider the efficient causes of all things: the proper ends and references of all actions: what pain is in itself; what pleasure, what death: what fame or honour, how every man is the true and proper ground of his own rest and tranquillity, and that no man can truly be hindered by any other: that all is but conceit and opinion. As for the use of thy dogmata, thou must carry thyself in the practice of them, rather like unto a pancratiastes, or one that at the same time both fights and wrestles with hands and feet, than a gladiator. For this, if he lose his sword that he fights with, he is gone: whereas the other hath still his hand free, which he may easily turn and manage at his will.

VII. All worldly things thou must behold and consider, dividing them into matter, form, and reference, or their proper end.

VIII. How happy is man in this his power that hath been granted unto him: that he needs not do anything but what God shall approve, and that he may embrace contentedly, whatsoever God doth send unto him?

IX. Whatsoever doth happen in the ordinary course and consequence of natural events, neither the Gods, (for it is not possible, that they either wittingly or unwittingly should do anything amiss) nor men, (for it is through ignorance, and therefore against their wills that they do anything amiss) must be accused. None then must be accused.

X. How ridiculous and strange is he, that wonders at anything that happens in this life in the ordinary course of nature!

XI. Either fate, (and that either an absolute necessity, and unavoidable decree; or a placable and flexible Providence) or all is a mere casual confusion, void of all order and government. If an absolute and unavoidable necessity, why doest thou resist? If a placable and exorable Providence, make thyself worthy of the divine help and assistance. If all be a mere confusion without any moderator, or governor, then hast thou reason to congratulate thyself; that in such a general flood of confusion thou thyself hast obtained a reasonable faculty, whereby thou mayest govern thine own life and actions. But if thou beest carried away with the flood, it must be thy body perchance, or thy life, or some other thing that belongs unto them that is carried away: thy mind and understanding cannot. Or should it be so, that the light of a candle indeed is still bright and lightsome until it be put out: and should truth, and righteousness, and temperance cease to shine in thee whilest thou thyself hast any being?

XII. At the conceit and apprehension that such and such a one hath sinned, thus reason with thyself; What do I know whether this be a sin indeed, as it seems to be? But if it be, what do I know but that he himself hath already condemned himself for it? And that is all one as if a man should scratch and tear his own face, an object of compassion rather than of anger. Again, that he that would not have a vicious man to sin, is like unto him that would not have moisture in the fig, nor children to welp nor a horse to neigh, nor anything else that in the course of nature is necessary. For what shall he do that hath such an habit? If thou therefore beest powerful and eloquent, remedy it if thou canst.

XIII. If it be not fitting, do it not. If it be not true, speak it not. Ever maintain thine own purpose and resolution free from all compulsion and necessity.

XIV. Of everything that presents itself unto thee, to consider what the true nature of it is, and to unfold it, as it were, by dividing it into that which is formal: that which is material: the true use or end of it, and the just time that it is appointed to last.

XV. It is high time for thee, to understand that there is somewhat in thee, better and more divine than either thy passions, or thy sensual appetites and affections. What is now the object of my mind, is it fear, or suspicion, or lust, or any such thing? To do nothing rashly without some certain end; let that be thy first care. The next, to have no other end than the common good. For, alas! yet a little while, and thou art no more: no more will any, either of those things that now thou seest, or of those men that now are living, be any more. For all things are by nature appointed soon to be changed, turned, and corrupted, that other things might succeed in their room.

XVI. Remember that all is but opinion, and all opinion depends of the mind. Take thine opinion away, and then as a ship that hath stricken in within the arms and mouth of the harbour, a present calm; all things safe and steady: a bay, not capable of any storms and tempests: as the poet hath it.

XVII. No operation whatsoever it he, ceasing for a while, can be truly said to suffer any evil, because it is at an end. Neither can he that is the author of that operation; for this very respect, because his operation is at an end, be said to suffer any evil. Likewise then, neither can the whole body of all our actions (which is our life) if in time it cease, be said to suffer any evil for this very reason, because it is at an end; nor he truly be said to have been ill affected, that did put a period to this series of actions. Now this time or certain period, depends of the determination of nature: sometimes of particular nature, as when a man dieth old; but of nature in general, however; the parts whereof thus changing one after another, the whole world still continues fresh and new. Now that is ever best and most seasonable, which is for the good of the whole. Thus it appears that death of itself can neither be hurtful to any in particular, because it is not a shameful thing (for neither is it a thing that depends of our own will, nor of itself contrary to the common good) and generally, as it is both expedient and seasonable to the whole, that in that respect it must needs be good. It is that also, which is brought unto us by the order and appointment of the Divine Providence; so that he whose will and mind in these things runs along with the Divine ordinance, and by this concurrence of his will and mind with the Divine Providence, is led and driven along, as it were by God Himself; may truly be termed and esteemed the θεοφόρητος, or divinely led and inspired.

XVIII. These three things thou must have always in a readiness: first concerning thine own actions, whether thou doest nothing either idly, or otherwise, than justice and equity do require: and concerning those things that happen unto thee externally, that either they happen unto thee by chance, or by providence; of which two to accuse either, is equally against reason. Secondly, what like unto our bodies are whilest yet rude and imperfect, until they be animated: and from their animation, until their expiration: of what things they are compounded, and into what things they shall be dissolved. Thirdly, how vain all things will appear unto thee when, from on high as it were, looking down thou shalt contemplate all things upon earth, and the wonderful mutability, that they are subject unto: considering withal, the infinite both greatness and variety of things aerial and things celestial that are round about it. And that as often as thou shalt behold them, thou shalt still see the same: as the same things, so the same shortness of continuance of all those things. And, behold, these be the things that we are so proud and puffed up for.

XIX. Cast away from thee opinion, and thou art safe. And what is it that hinders thee from casting of it away? When thou art grieved at anything, hast thou forgotten that all things happen according to the nature of the universe; and that him only it concerns, who is in fault; and moreover, that what is now done, is that which from ever hath been done in the world, and will ever be done, and is now done everywhere: how nearly all men are allied one to another by a kindred not of blood, nor of seed, but of the same mind. Thou hast also forgotten that every man's mind partakes of the Deity, and issueth from thence; and that no man can properly call anything his own, no not his son, nor his body, nor his life; for that they all proceed from that One who is the giver of all things: that all things are but opinion; that no man lives properly, but that very instant of time which is now present. And therefore that no man whensoever he dieth can properly be said to lose any more, than an instant of time.

XX. Let thy thoughts ever run upon them, who once for some one thing or other, were moved with extraordinary indignation; who were once in the highest pitch of either honour, or calamity; or mutual hatred and enmity; or of any other fortune or condition whatsoever. Then consider what's now become of all those things. All is turned to smoke; all to ashes, and a mere fable; and perchance not so much as a fable. As also whatsoever is of this nature, as Fabius Catulinus in the field; Lucius Lupus, and Stertinius, at Baiæ Tiberius at Capreæ and Velius Rufus, and all such examples of vehement prosecution in worldly matters; let these also run in thy mind at the same time; and how vile every object of such earnest and vehement prosecution is; and how much more agreeable to true philosophy it is, for a man to carry himself in every matter that offers itself; justly, and moderately, as one that followeth the Gods with all simplicity. For, for a man to be proud and high conceited, that he is not proud and high conceited, is of all kind of pride and presumption, the most intolerable.

XXI. To them that ask thee, Where hast thou seen the Gods, or how knowest thou certainly that there be Gods, that thou art so devout in their worship? I answer first of all, that even to the very eye, they are in some manner visible and apparent. Secondly, neither have I ever seen mine own soul, and yet I respect and honour it. So then for the Gods, by the daily experience that I have of their power and providence towards myself and others, I know certainly that they are, and therefore worship them.

XXII. Herein doth consist happiness of life, for a man to know thoroughly the true nature of everything; what is the matter, and what is the form of it: with all his heart and soul, ever to do that which is just, and to speak the truth. What then remaineth but to enjoy thy life in a course and coherence of good actions, one upon another immediately succeeding, and never interrupted, though for never so little a while?

XXIII. There is but one light of the sun, though it be intercepted by walls and mountains, and other thousand objects. There is but one common substance of the whole world, though it be concluded and restrained into several different bodies, in number infinite. There is but one common soul, though divided into innumerable particular essences and natures. So is there but one common intellectual soul, though it seem to be divided. And as for all other parts of those generals which we have mentioned, as either sensitive souls or subjects, these of themselves (as naturally irrational) have no common mutual reference one unto another, though many of them contain a mind, or reasonable faculty in them, whereby they are ruled and governed. But of every reasonable mind, this the particular nature, that it hath reference to whatsoever is of her own kind, and desireth to be united: neither can this common affection, or mutual unity and correspondency, be here intercepted or divided, or confined to particulars as those other common things are.

XXIV. What doest thou desire? To live long. What? To enjoy the operations of a sensitive soul; or of the appetitive faculty? or wouldst thou grow, and then decrease again? Wouldst thou long be able to talk, to think and reason with thyself? Which of all these seems unto thee a worthy object of thy desire? Now if of all these thou doest find that they be but little worth in themselves, proceed on unto the last, which is, in all things to follow God and reason. But for a man to grieve that by death he shall be deprived of any of these things, is both against God and reason.

XXV. What a small portion of vast and infinite eternity it is, that is allowed unto every one of us, and how soon it vanisheth into the general age of the world: of the common substance, and of the common soul also what a small portion is allotted unto us: and in what a little clod of the whole earth (as it were) it is that thou doest crawl. After thou shalt rightly have considered these things with thyself; fancy not anything else in the world any more to be of any weight and moment but this, to do that only which thine own nature doth require; and to conform thyself to that which the common nature doth afford.

XXVI. What is the present estate of my understanding? For herein lieth all indeed. As for all other things, they are without the compass of mine own will: and if without the compass of my will, then are they as dead things unto me, and as it were mere smoke.

XXVII. To stir up a man to the contempt of death this among other things, is of good power and efficacy, that even they who esteemed pleasure to be happiness, and pain misery, did nevertheless many of them contemn death as much as any. And can death be terrible to him, to whom that only seems good, which in the ordinary course of nature is seasonable? to him, to whom, whether his actions be many or few, so they be all good, is all one; and who whether he behold the things of the world being always the same either for many years, or for few years only, is altogether indifferent? O man! as a citizen thou hast lived, and conversed in this great city the world. Whether just for so many years, or no, what is it unto thee? Thou hast lived (thou mayest be sure) as long as the laws and orders of the city required; which may be the common comfort of all. Why then should it be grievous unto thee, if (not a tyrant, nor an unjust judge, but) the same nature that brought thee in, doth now send thee out of the world? As if the praetor should fairly dismiss him from the stage, whom he had taken in to act a while. Oh, but the play is not yet at an end, there are but three acts yet acted of it? Thou hast well said: for in matter of life, three acts is the whole play. Now to set a certain time to every man's acting, belongs unto him only, who as first he was of thy composition, so is now the cause of thy dissolution. As for thyself; thou hast to do with neither. Go thy ways then well pleased and contented: for so is He that dismisseth thee.

APPENDIX

CORRESPONDENCE OF M. AURELIUS ANTONINUS AND M. CORNELIUS FRONTO[1]

M. CORNELIUS FRONTO was a Roman by descent, but of provincial birth, being native to Cirta, in Numidia. Thence he migrated to Rome in the reign of Hadrian, and became the most famous rhetorician of his day. As a pleader and orator he was counted by his contemporaries hardly inferior to Tully himself, and as a teacher his aid was sought for the noblest youths of Rome. To him was entrusted the education of M.

Aurelius and of his colleague L. Verus in their boyhood; and he was rewarded for his efforts by a seat in the Senate and the consular rank (A.D. 143). By the exercise of his profession he became wealthy; and if he speaks of his means as not great,[2] he must be comparing his wealth with the grandees of Rome, not with the ordinary citizen.

Before the present century nothing was known of the works of Fronto, except a grammatical treatise; but in 1815 Cardinal Mai published a number of letters and some short essays of Fronto, which he had discovered in a palimpsest at Milan. Other parts of the same MS. he found later in the Vatican, the whole being collected

Meditations

[1] References are made to the edition of Naber, Leipzig (Trübner), 1867.

[2] Ad Verum imp. Aur. Caes., ii, 7. and edited in the year 1823.

We now possess parts of his correspondence with Antoninus Pius, with M. Aurelius, with L. Verus, and with certain of his friends, and also several rhetorical and historical fragments. Though none of the more ambitious works of Fronto have survived, there are enough to give proof of his powers. Never was a great literary reputation less deserved. It would be hard to conceive of anything more vapid than the style and conception of these letters; clearly the man was a pedant without imagination or taste. Such indeed was the age he lived in, and it is no marvel that he was like to his age. But there must have been more in him than mere pedantry; there was indeed a heart in the man, which Marcus found, and he found also a tongue which could speak the truth. Fronto's letters are by no means free from exaggeration and laudation, but they do not show that loathsome flattery which filled the Roman court. He really admires what he praises, and his way of saying so is not unlike what often passes for criticism at the present day. He is not afraid to reprove what he thinks amiss; and the astonishment of Marcus at this will prove, if proof were needed, that he was not used to plain dealing. "How happy I am," he writes, "that my friend Marcus Cornelius, so distinguished as an orator and so noble as a man, thinks me worth praising and blaming."[3] In another place he deems himself blest because Fronto had taught him to speak the truth[4] although the context shows him to be speaking of expression, it is still a point in favour of Fronto. A sincere heart is better than literary taste; and if Fronto had not done his duty by the young prince, it is not easy to understand the friendship which remained between them up to the last.

[3] Ad M. Caes iii. 17

[4] Ad M. Caes iii. 12

An example of the frankness which was between them is given by a difference they had over the case of Herodes Atticus. Herodes was a Greek rhetorician who had a school at Rome, and Marcus Aurelius was among his pupils. Both Marcus and the Emperor Antoninus had a high opinion of Herodes; and all we know goes to prove he was a man of high character and princely generosity. When quite young he was made administrator of the free cities in Asia, nor is it surprising to find that he made bitter enemies there; indeed, a just ruler was sure to make enemies. The end of it was that an Athenian deputation, headed by the orators Theodotus and Demostratus, made serious accusations against his honour. There is no need to discuss the merits of the case here; suffice it to say, Herodes succeeded in defending himself to the satisfaction of the emperor. Pronto appears to have taken the delegates' part, and to have accepted a brief for the prosecution, urged to some extent by personal considerations; and in this cause Marcus Aurelius writes to Fronto as follows:—

'AURELIUS CÆSAR to his friend FRONTO, greeting.[5]

'I know you have often told me you were anxious to find how you might best please me. Now is the time; now you can increase my love towards you, if it can be increased. A trial is at hand, in which people seem likely not only to hear your speech with pleasure, but to see your indignation with impatience. I see no one who dares give you a hint in the matter; for those who are less friendly, prefer to see you act with some inconsistency; and those who are more friendly, fear to seem too friendly to your opponent if they should dissuade you from your accusation; then again, in case you have prepared something neat for the occasion, they cannot endure to rob you of your harangue by silencing you. Therefore, whether you think me a rash counsellor, or a bold boy, or too kind to your opponent, not because I think it better, I will offer my counsel with some caution. But why have I said, offer my counsel? No, I demand it from you; I demand it boldly, and if I succeed, I promise to remain under your obligation. What? you will say if I am attackt, shall I not pay tit for tat? Ah, but you will get greater glory, if even when attackt you answer nothing. Indeed, if he begins it, answer as you will and you will have fair excuse; but I have demanded of him that he shall not begin, and I think I have succeeded. I love each of you according to your merits and I know that lie was educated in the house of P. Calvisius, my grandfather, and that I was educated by you; therefore I am full of anxiety that this most disagreeable business shall be managed as honourably as possible. I trust you may approve my advice, for my intention you will approve. At least I prefer to write unwisely rather than to be silent unkindly.'

[5] Ad M. Caes ii., 2.

Fronto replied, thanking the prince for his advice, and promising that he will confine himself to the facts of the case. But he points out that the charges brought against Herodes were such, that they can hardly be made agreeable; amongst them being spoliation, violence, and murder. However, he is willing even to let some of these drop if it be the prince's pleasure. To this Marcus returned the following answer:—[6] 'This one thing, my dearest Fronto, is enough to make me truly grateful to you, that so far from rejecting my counsel, you have even approved it. As to the question you raise in your kind letter, my opinion is this: all that concerns the case which you are supporting must be clearly brought forward; what concerns your own feelings, though you may have had just provocation, should be left unsaid.' The story does credit to both. Fronto shows no loss of temper at the interference, nor shrinks from stating his case with frankness; and Marcus, with forbearance remarkable in a prince, does not command that his friend be left unmolested, but merely stipulates for a fair trial on the merits of the case.

[6] Ad. M. Caes., iii. 5.

Another example may be given from a letter of Fronto's[7] Here is something else quarrelsome and querulous. I have sometimes found fault with you in your absence somewhat seriously in the company of a few of my most intimate friends: at times, for example, when you mixt in society with a more solemn look than was fitting, or would read books in the theatre or in a banquet; nor did I absent myself from theatre or banquet when you did.[8] Then I used to call you a hard man, no good company, even disagreeable, sometimes, when anger got the better of me. But did any one else in the same banquet speak against you, I could not endure to hear it with equanimity. Thus it was easier for me to say something to your disadvantage myself, than to hear others do it; just as I could more easily bear to chastise my daughter Gratia, than to see her chastised by another.'

216

[7] Ad. M. Caes., iv. 12.

[8] The text is obscure

The affection between them is clear from every page of the correspondence. A few instances are now given, which were written at different periods

To MY MASTER.[9]

'This is how I have past the last few days. My sister was suddenly seized with an internal pain, so violent that I was horrified at her looks; my mother in her trepidation on that account accidentally bruised her side on a corner of the wall; she and we were greatly troubled about that blow. For myself; on going to rest I found a scorpion in my bed; but I did not lie down upon him, I killed him first. If you are getting on better, that is a consolation. My mother is easier now, thanks be to God. Good-bye, best and sweetest master. My lady sends you greeting.'

[9] Ad M. Caes., v. 8.

[10]'What words can I find to fit my had luck, or how shall I upbraid as it deserves the hard constraint which is laid upon me? It ties me fast here, troubled my heart is, and beset by such anxiety; nor does it allow me to make haste to my Fronto, my life and delight, to be near him at such a moment of ill-health in particular, to hold his hands, to chafe gently that identical foot, so far as may be done without discomfort, to attend him in the bath, to support his steps with my arm.'

[10] Ad M. Caes., i. 2.

[11]'This morning I did not write to you, because I heard you were better, and because I was myself engaged

in other business, and I cannot ever endure to write anything to you unless with mind at ease and untroubled and free. So if we are all right, let me know: what I desire, you know, and how properly I desire it, I know. Farewell, my master, always in every chance first in my mind, as you deserve to be. My master, see I am not asleep, and I compel myself to sleep, that you may not be angry with me. You gather I am writing this late at night.'

[11] iii. 21.

[12]'What spirit do you suppose is in me, when I remember how long it is since I have seen you, and why I have not seen you! and it may be I shall not see you for a few days yet, while you are strengthening yourself; as you must. So while you lie on the sick-bed, my spirit also will lie low anti, whenas,[13] by God's mercy you shall stand upright, my spirit too will stand firm, which is now burning with the strongest desire for you. Farewell, soul of your prince, your pupil.'

[14]O my dear Fronto, most distinguished Consul! I yield, you have conquered: all who have ever loved before, you have conquered out and out in love's contest. Receive the victor's wreath; and the herald shall proclaim your victory aloud before your own tribunal: "M. Cornelius Fronto, Consul, wins, and is crowned victor in the Open International Love-race."[15] But beaten though I may be, I shall neither slacken nor relax my own zeal. Well, you shall love me more than any man loves any other man; but I, who possess a faculty of loving less strong, shall love you more than any one else loves you; more indeed than you love yourself. Gratia and I will have to fight for it; I doubt I shall not get the better of her. For,

as Plautus says, her love is like rain, whose big drops not only penetrate the dress, but drench to the very marrow.'

[12] Ad M. Caes., iii. 19.

[13] The writer sometimes uses archaisms such as *quom*, which I render 'whenas'.

[14] Ad M. Caes., ii. 2.

[15] The writer parodies the proclamation at the Greek games; the words also are Greek.

Marcus Aurelius seems to have been about eighteen years of age when the correspondence begins, Fronto being some thirty years older.[16] The systematic education of the young prince seems to have been finisht, and Pronto now acts more as his adviser than his tutor. He recommends the prince to use simplicity in his public speeches, and to avoid affectation.[17] Marcus devotes his attention to the old authors who then had a great vogue at Rome: Ennius, Plautus, Nævius, and such orators as Cato and Gracchus.[18] Pronto urges on him the study of Cicero, whose letters, he says, are all worth reading.

[16] From internal evidence: the letters are not arranged in order of time. See Naher's *Prolegomena*, p. xx. foll.

[17] Ad M. Caes., iii. x.

[18] Ad M. Caes ii. 10,; iii. 18,; ii. 4.

When he wishes to compliment Marcus he declares one or other of his letters has the true Tullian ring. Marcus gives his nights to reading when he ought to be sleeping.

He exercises himself in verse composition and on rhetorical themes.

'It is very nice of you,' he writes to Fronto,[19] 'to ask for my hexameters; I would have sent them at once if I had them by me. The fact is my secretary, Anicetus-you know who I mean-did not pack up any of my compositions for me to take away with me. He knows my weakness; he was afraid that if I got hold of them I might, as usual, make smoke of them. However, there was no fear for the hexameters. I must confess the truth to my master: I love them. I study at night, since the day is taken up with the theatre. I am weary of an evening, and sleepy in the daylight, and so I don't do much. Yet I have made extracts from sixty books, five volumes of them, in these latter days. But when you read remember that the "sixty" includes plays of Novius, and farces, and some little speeches of Scipio; don't be too much startled at the number. You remember your Polemon; but I pray you do not remember Horace, who has died with Pollio as far as I am concerned.[20] Farewell, my dearest and most affectionate friend, most distinguished consul and my beloved master, whom I have not seen these two years. Those who say two months, count the days. Shall I ever see you again?'

[19] Ad M. Caes., ii. 10.

[20] He implies, as in i. 6, that he has ceased to study Horace.

Sometimes Fronto sends him a theme to work up, as thus: 'M. Lucilius tribune of the people violently throws into prison a free Roman citizen, against the opinion of his colleagues who demand his release. For this act he is branded by the censor. Analyse the case, and then take both sides in turn, attacking and defending.'[21] Or again: 'A Roman consul, doffing his state robe, dons the gauntlet and kills a lion amongst the young men at the Quinquatrus in full view of the people of Rome. Denunciation before the censors.'[22] The prince has a fair knowledge of Greek, and quotes from Homer, Plato, Euripides, but for some reason Fronto dissuaded him from this study.[23] His *Meditations* are written in Greek. He continued his literary studies throughout his life, and after he became emperor we still find him asking his adviser for copies of Cicero's Letters, by which he hopes to improve his vocabulary.[24] Pronto helps him with a supply of similes, which, it seems, he did not think of readily. It is to be feared that the fount of Marcus's eloquence was pumped up by artificial means.

[21] Pollio was a grammarian, who taught Marcus.

[22] Ad M. Caes., v. 27,; V. 22.

[23] Ep. Gracae, 6.

[24] Ad Anton. Imp., II. 4.

Some idea of his literary style may be gathered from the letter which follows:[25]

'I heard Polemo declaim the other day, to say something of things sublunary. If you ask what I thought of him, listen. He seems to me an industrious farmer, endowed with the greatest skill, who has cultivated a large estate for corn and vines only, and indeed with a rich return of fine crops. But yet in that land of his there is no Pompeian fig or Arician vegetable, no Tarentine rose, or pleasing coppice, or thick grove, or shady plane tree; all is for use rather than for pleasure, such as one ought rather to commend, but cares not to love.

[25] Ad M. Caes, ii. 5.

A pretty bold idea, is it not, and rash judgment, to pass censure on a man of such reputation? But whenas I remember that I am writing to you, I think I am less bold than you would have me.

'In that point I am wholly undecided.

'There's an unpremeditated hendecasyllable for you. So before I begin to poetize, I'll take an easy with you. Farewell, my heart's desire, your Verus's best beloved, most distinguisht consul, master most sweet. Farewell I ever pray, sweetest soul.

What a letter do you think you have written me I could make bold to say, that never did she who bore me and nurst me, write anything SO delightful, so honey-sweet. And this does not come of your fine style and eloquence: otherwise not my mother only, but all who breathe.'

To the pupil, never was anything on earth so fine as his master's eloquence; on this theme Marcus fairly bubbles over with enthusiasm.

[26]'Well, if the ancient Greeks ever wrote anything like this, let those who know decide it: for me, if I dare say so, I never read any invective of Cato's so fine as your encomtum. O if my Lord[27] could be sufficiently praised, sufficiently praised he would have been undoubtedly by you! This kind of thing is not done nowadays.[28] It were easier to match Pheidias, easier to match Apelles, easier

Meditations

in a word to match Demosthenes himself, or Cato himself; than to match this finisht and perfect work. Never have I read anything more refined, anything more after the ancient type, anything more delicious, anything more Latin. O happy you, to be endowed with eloquence so great! O happy I, to be tinder the charge of such a master! O arguments,[29] O arrangement, O elegance, O wit, O beauty, O words, O brilliancy, O subtilty, O grace, O treatment, O everything! Mischief take me, if you ought not to have a rod put in your hand one day, a diadem on your brow, a tribunal raised for you; then the herald would summon us all-why do I say "us"? Would summnon all, those scholars and orators: one by one you would beckon them forward with your rod and admonish them. Hitherto I have had no fear of this admonition; many things help me to enter within your school. I write this in the utmost haste; for whenas I am sending you so kindly a letter from my Lord, what needs a longer letter of mine? Farewell then, glory of Roman eloquence, boast of your friends, magnifico, most delightful man, most distinguished consul, master most sweet.

[26] Ad M. Caes., ii. 3.

[27] The Emperor Antoninus Pius is spoken of as *dominus meus*.

[28] This sentence is written in Greek.

[29] Several of these words are Greek, and the meaning is not quite clear.

'After this you will take care not to tell so many fibs of me, especially in the Senate. A monstrous fine speech this is! O if I could kiss your head at every heading of it! You have looked down on all with a vengeance. This oration once read, in vain shall we study, in vain shall we toil, in vain strain every nerve. Farewell always, most sweet master.'

Sometimes Fronto descends from the heights of eloquence to offer practical advice; as when he suggests how Marcus should deal with his suite. It is more difficult, he admits, to keep courtiers in harmony than to tame lions with a lute; but if it is to be done, it must be by eradicating jealousy. 'Do not let your friends,' says Fronto,'[30] 'envy each other, or think that what you give to another is filched from them.

[30] Ad M Caes., iv. 1.

Keep away envy from your suite, and you will find your friends kindly and harmonious.'

Here and there we meet with allusions to his daily life, which we could wish to be more frequent. He goes to the theatre or the law-courts,[31] or takes part in court ceremony, but his heart is always with his books. The vintage season, with its religious rites, was always spent by Antoninus Pius in the country. The following letters give sonic notion of a day's occupation at that time:[32]

[31] ii. 14

[32] iv. 5,6.

'MY DEAREST MASTER,—I am well. To-day I studied from the ninth hour of the night to the second hour of day, after taking food. I then put on my slippers, and from time second to the third hour had a most enjoyable walk up and down before my chamber. Then booted and cloaked-for so we were commanded to appear-I went to

Meditations

wait upon my lord the emperor. We went a-hunting, did doughty deeds, heard a rumour that boars had been caught, but there was nothing to see. However, we climbed a pretty steep hill, and in the afternoon returned home. I went straight to my books. Off with the boots, down with the cloak; I spent a couple of hours in bed. I read Cato's speech on the Property of Pulchra, and another in which he impeaches a tribune. Ho, ho! I hear you cry to your man, Off with you as fast as you can, and bring me these speeches from the library of Apollo. No use to send: I have those books with me too. You must get round the Tiberian librarian; you will have to spend something on the matter; and when I return to town, I shall expect to go shares with him. Well, after reading these speeches I wrote a wretched trifle, destined for drowning or burning. No, indeed my attempt at writing did not come off at all to-day; the composition of a hunter or a vintager, whose shouts are echoing through my chamber, hateful and wearisome as the law-courts. What have I said? Yes, it was rightly said, for my master is an orator. I think I have caught cold, whether from walking in slippers or from writing badly, I do not know. I am always annoyed with phlegm, but to-day I seem to snivel more than usual. Well, I will pour oil on my head and go off to sleep. I don't mean to put one drop in my lamp to-day, so weary am I from riding and sneezing. Farewell, dearest and most beloved master, whom I miss, I may say, more than Rome itself.'

'MY BELOVED MASTER,-I am well. I slept a little more than usual for my slight cold, which seems to be well again. So I spent the time from the eleventh hour of the night to the third of the day partly in reading in Cato's Agriculture, partly in writing, not quite so badly as yesterday indeed. Then, after waiting upon my father, I soothed my throat with honey-water, ejecting it without swallowing: I might say *gargle*, but I won't, though I think the word is found in Novius and elsewhere. After attending to my throat I went to my father, and stood by his side as he sacrificed. Then to luncheon. What do you think I had to eat? A bit of bread so big, while I watched others gobbling boiled beans, onions, and fish full of roe. Then we set to work at gathering the grapes, with plenty of sweat and shouting, and, as the quotation runs, "A few high-hanging clusters did we leave survivors of the vintage." After the sixth hour we returned home. I did a little work, and poor work at that. Then I had a long gossip with my dear mother sitting on the bed. My conversation was: What do you think my friend Fronto is doing just now? She said: And what do you think of my friend Gratia?'[33] My turn now: And what of our little Gratia,[34] the sparrowkin? After this kind of talk, and an argument as to which of you loved the other most, the gong sounded, the signal that my father had gone to the bath. We supped, after ablutions in the oil-cellar-I mean we supped after ablutions, not after ablutions in the oil-cellar; and listened with enjoyment to the rustics gibing. After returning, before turning on my side to snore, I do my task and give an account of the day to my delightful master, whom if I could long for a little more, I should not mind growing a trifle thinner. Farewell, Fronto, wherever you are, honey-sweet, my darling, my delight. Why do I want you? I can love you while far away.'

[33] Fronto's wife.

[34] Fronto's daughter

One anecdote puts Marcus before us in a new light:[35]

Meditations

[35] Ad M. Caes ii. 12.

'When my father returned home from the vineyards, I mounted my horse as usual, and rode on ahead some little way. Well, there on the road was a herd of sheep, standing all crowded together as though the place were a desert, with four dogs and two shepherds, but nothing else. Then one shepherd said to another shepherd, on seeing a number of horsemen: 'I say,' says he, 'look you at those horsemen; they do a deal of robbery.' When I heard this, I clap spurs to my horse, and ride straight for the sheep. In consternation the sheep scatter; hither and thither they are fleeting and bleating. A shepherd throws his fork, and the fork falls on the horseman who came next to me. We make our escape.' We like Marcus none the worse for this spice of mischief.

Another letter[36] describes a visit to a country town, and shows the antiquarian spirit of the writer:—

'M. CÆSAR to his MASTER M. FRONTO, greeting.

'After I entered the carriage, after I took leave of you, we made a journey comfortable enough, but we had a few drops of rain to wet us. But before coming to the country-house, we broke our journey at Anagnia, a mile or so from the highroad. Then we inspected that ancient town, a miniature it is, but has in it many antiquities, temples, and religious ceremonies quite out of the way. There is not a corner without its shrine, or fane, or temple; besides, many books written on linen, which belongs to things sacred. Then on the gate as we came out was written twice, as follows: "Priest don the fell."[37] I asked one of the inhabitants what that word was. He said it was the word in the Hernican dialect for the victim's skin, which the priest puts over his conical cap when he enters the city. I found out many other things which I desired to know, but the only thing I do not desire is that you should be absent from me; that is my chief anxiety. Now for yourself, when you left that place, did you go to Aurelia or to Campania? Be sure to write to me, and say whether you have opened the vintage, or carried a host of books to the country-house; this also, whether you miss me; I am foolish to ask it, whenas you tell it me of yourself. Now if you miss me and if you love me, send me your letters often, which is a comfort and consolation to me. Indeed I should prefer ten times to read your letters than all the vines of Gaurus or the Marsians; for these Signian vines have grapes too rank and fruit too sharp in the taste, but I prefer wine to must for drinking. Besides, those grapes are nicer to eat dried than fresh-ripe; I vow I would rather tread them under foot than put my teeth in them. But I pray they may be gracious and forgiving, and grant me free pardon for these jests of mine. Farewell, best friend, dearest, most learned, sweetest master. When you see the must ferment in the vat, remember that just so in my heart the longing for you is gushing and flowing and bubbling. Good-bye.'

[36] Ad Verum. Imp ii. 1, s. fin.

[37] Santentum

Making all allowances for conventional exaggerations, it is clear from the correspondence that there was deep love between Marcus and his preceptor. The letters cover several years in succession, but soon after the birth of Marcus's daughter, Faustina, there is a large gap. It does not follow that the letters ceased entirely, because we know part of the collection is lost;

but there was probably less intercourse between Marcus and Fronto after Marcus took to the study of philosophy under the guidance of Rusticus.

When Marcus succeeded to the throne in 161, the letters begin again, with slightly increased formality on Fronto's part, and they go on for some four years, when Fronto, who has been continually complaining of ill-health, appears to have died. One letter of the later period gives some interesting particulars of the emperor's public life, which are worth quoting. Fronto speaks of Marcus's victories and eloquence in the usual strain of high praise, and then continues.[38]

'The army when you took it in hand was sunk in luxury and revelry, and corrupted with long inactivity. At Antiochia the soldiers had been wont to applaud at the stage plays, knew more of the gardens at the nearest restaurant than of the battlefield. Horses were hairy from lack of grooming, horsemen smooth because their hairs had been pulled out by the roots[39] a rare thing it was to see a soldier with hair on arm or leg. Moreover, they were better drest than armed; so much so, that Laelianus Pontius, a strict man of the old discipline, broke the cuirasses of some of them with his finger-tips, and observed cushions on the horses' backs. At his direction the tufts were cut through, and out of the horsemen's saddles came what appeared to be feathers pluckt from geese. Few of the men could vault on horseback, the rest clambered up with difficulty by aid of heel and knee and leg not many could throw a lance hurtling, most did it without force or power, as though they were things of wool-dicing was common in the camp, sleep lasted all night, or if they kept watch it was over the winecup. By what regulations to restrain such soldiers as these, and to turn them to honesty and industry, did you not learn from Hannibal's sternness, the discipline of Africanus, the acts of Metellus recorded in history.

[38] Ad Verum. imp., ii. I, s.fin.

[39] A common mark of the effeminate at Rome.

After the preceptorial letters cease the others are concerned with domestic events, health and sickness, visits or introductions, birth or death. Thus the empperor writes to his old friend, who had shown some diffidence in seeking an interview:[40]

[40] Ad Verum. Imp. Aur. Caes., i. 3.

'To MY MASTER.

'I have a serious grievance against you, my dear master, yet indeed my grief is more than my grievance, because after so long a time I neither embraced you nor spoke to you, though you visited the palace, and the moment after I had left the prince my brother. I reproached my brother severely for not recalling me; nor durst he deny the fault.' Fronto again writes on one occasion: 'I have seen your daughter. It was like seeing you and Faustina in infancy, so much that is charming her face has taken from each of yours.' Or again, at a later date:[41] I have seen your chicks, most delightful sight that ever I saw in my life, so like you that nothing is more like than the likeness.... By the mercy of Heaven they have a healthy colour and strong lungs. One held a piece of white bread, like a little prince, the other a common piece, like a true philosophers son.'

[41] Ad Ant. Imp i., 3.

Marcus, we know, was devoted to his children. They were delicate in health, in spite of Fronto's assurance, and only one son survived the father. We find echoes of this affection now and again in the letters. 'We have summer heat here still,' writes Marcus, 'but since my little girls are pretty well, if I may say so, it is like the bracing climate of spring to us.'[42] When little Faustina came back from the valley of the shadow of death, her father at once writes to inform Fronto.[43] The sympathy he asks he also gives, and as old age brings more and more infirmity, Marcus becomes even more solicitous for his beloved teacher. The poor old man suffered a heavy blow in the death of his grandson, on which Marcus writes:[44] 'I have just heard of your misfortune. Feeling grieved as I do when one of your joints gives you pain, what do you think I feel, dear master, when you have pain of mind?' The old man's reply, in spite of a certain self-consciousness, is full of pathos. He recounts with pride the events of a long and upright life, in which he has wronged no man, and lived in harmony with his friends and family. His affectations fall away from him, as the cry of pain is forced from his heart:—

[42] Ad M. Caes., v. 19

[43] iv. 11

[44] De Nepote Amissa

[45]'Many such sorrows has fortune visited me with all my life long. To pass by my other afflictions, I have lost five children under the most pitiful conditions possible: for the five I lost one by one when each was my only child, suffering these blows of bereavement in such a manner that each child was born to one already

bereaved. Thus I ever lost my children without solace, and got them amidst fresh grief.....'

[45] De Nepote Amissa 2

The letter continues with reflections on the nature of death, 'more to be rejoiced at than bewailed, the younger one dies,' and an arraignment of Providence not without dignity, wrung from him as it were by this last culminating misfortune. It concludes with a summing-up of his life in protest against the blow which has fallen on his grey head.

'Through my long life I have committed nothing which might bring dishonour, or disgrace, or shame: no deed of avarice or treachery have I done in all my day's: nay, but much generosity, much kindness, much truth and faithfulness have I shown, often at the risk of my own life. I have lived in amity with my good brother, whom I rejoice to see in possession of the highest office by your father's goodness, and by your friendship at peace and perfect rest. The offices which I have myself obtained I never strove for by any underhand means. I have cultivated my mind rather than my body; the pursuit of learning I have preferred to increasing my wealth. I preferred to be poor rather than bound by any' man's obligation, even to want rather than to beg. I have never been extravagant in spending money, I have earned it sometimes because I must. I have scrupulously spoken the truth, and have been glad to hear it spoken to me. I have thought it better to be neglected than to fawn, to be dumb than to feign, to be seldom a friend than to be often a flatterer. I have sought little, deserved not little. So far as I could, I have assisted each according to my means. I have given help readily to the deserving, fearlessly to the undeserving. No one by proving to be ungrateful has made me more slow to bestow promptly all benefits I could give, nor have I ever been harsh to ingratitude. (A fragmentary passage follows, in which he appears to speak of his desire for a peaceful end, and the desolation of his house.) I have suffered long and painful sickness, my beloved Marcus. Then I was visited by pitiful misfortunes: my wife I have lost, my grandson I have lost in Germany:[46] woe is me! I have lost my Decimanus. If I were made of iron, at this tine I could write no more.'

[46] In the war against the Catti.

It is noteworthy that in his *Meditations* Marcus Aurelius mentions Fronto only once.[47] All his literary studies, his oratory and criticism (such as it was) is forgotten; and, says he, 'Fronto taught me not to expect natural affection from the highly-born.' Fronto really said more than this: that 'affection' is not a Roman quality, nor has it a Latin name.[48] Roman or not Roman, Marcus found affection in Fronto; and if he outgrew his master's intellectual training, he never lost touch with the true heart of the man it is that which Fronto's name brings up to his remembrance, not dissertations on compound verbs or fatuous criticisms of style.

[47] Book I., 8.

[48] Ad Verum, ii. 7

NOTES

This being neither a critical edition of the text nor an emended edition of Casaubon's translation, it has not been thought necessary to add full notes. Casaubon's own notes have been omitted, because for the most part they are discursive, and not necessary to an understanding of what is written. In those which here follow, certain emendations of his are mentioned, which he proposes in his notes, and follows in the translation. In addition, one or two corrections are made where he has mistaken the Greek, and the translation might be misleading. Those which do not come under these two heads will explain themselves.

The text itself has been prepared by a comparison of the editions of 1634 and 1635. It should be borne in mind that Casaubon's is often rather a paraphrase than a close translation; and it did not seem worth while to notice every variation or amplification of the original. In the original editions all that Casaubon conceives as understood, but not expressed, is enclosed in square brackets. These brackets are here omitted, as they interfere with the comfort of the reader; and so have some of the alternative renderings suggested by the translator. In a few cases, Latin words in the text have been replaced by English.

Numbers in brackets refer to the Teubner text of Stich, but the divisions of the text are left unaltered. For some of the references identified I am indebted to Mr. G. H. Rendall's *Marcus Aurelius*.

BOOK II "Both to frequent" (4). Gr. τὸ μή, C. conjectures τὸ μὲ. The text is probably right: "I did not frequent public lectures, and I was taught at home."

VI Idiots.... philosophers (9). The reading is doubtful, but the meaning seems to be: "simple and unlearned men"

XII "Claudius Maximus" (15). The reading of the Palatine MS. (now lost) was paraklhsiz Maximon, which C. supposes to conceal the letters kl as an abbreviation of Claudius.

XIII "Patient hearing... He would not" (16). C. translates his conjectural reading epimonon ollan. on proapsth Stich suggests a reading with much the same sense: .....epimonon all antoi "Strict and rigid dealing" (16). C. translates tonvn (Pal. MS.) as though from tonoz, in the sense of "strain." "rigour." The reading of other MSS. tonvn is preferable.

XIII "Congiaries" (13). dianomais, "doles."

XIV "Cajeta" (17). The passage is certainly corrupt. C. spies a reference to Chryses praying by the sea-shore in the Illiad, and supposes M. Aurelius to have done the like. None of the emendations suggested is satisfactory. At § XV. Book II. is usually reckoned to begin. BOOK II III. "Do, soul" (6). If the received reading be right, it must be sarcastic; but there are several variants which show how unsatisfactory it is. C. translates "en gar o bioz ekasty so par eanty", which I do not understand. The sense required is: "Do not violence to thyself, for thou hast not long to use self-respect. Life is not (v. 1. so long for each, and this life for thee is all but done."

X. "honour and credit do proceed" (12). The verb has dropt out of the text, but C. has supplied one of the required meaning.

XI. "Consider," etc. (52). This verb is not in the Greek, which means: "(And reason also shows) how man, etc."

BOOK IV XV. "Agathos" (18): This is probably not a proper name, but the text seems to be unsound. The meaning may be "the good man ought"

XVI. oikonomian (16) is a "practical benefit," a secondary end. XXXIX. "For herein lieth all...." (~3). C. translates his conjecture olan for ola.

BOOK V XIV. katorqwseiz (15): Acts of "rightness" or "straightness." XXIII. "Roarer" (28): Gr. "tragedian." Ed. 1 has whoremonger,' ed. 2 corrects to "harlot," but omits to alter' the word at its second occurrence.

XXV. "Thou hast... them" (33): A quotation from Homer, Odyssey, iv. 690.

XXVII. "One of the poets" (33): Hesiod, Op. et Dies, 197.

XXIX and XXX. (36). The Greek appears to contain quotations from sources not known, and the translation is a paraphrase. (One or two alterations are here made on the authority of the second edition.) BOOK VI XIII. "Affected and qualified" (i4): exis, the power of cohesion

Meditations

shown in things inanimate; fusiz, power of growth seen in plants and the like.

XVII. "Wonder at them" (18): i.e. mankind.

XXXVII. "Chrysippus" (42): C. refers to a passage of Plutarch De Communibus Notitiis (c. xiv.), where Chrysippus is represented as saying that a coarse phrase may be vile in itself, yet have due place in a comedy as contributing to a certain effect.

XL. "Man or men..." There is no hiatus in the Greek, which means: "Whatever (is beneficial) for a man is so for other men also."

XLII. There is no hiatus in the Greek.

BOOK VII IX. C. translates his conjecture mh for h. The Greek means "straight, or rectified," with a play on the literal and metaphorical meaning of ortoz.

XIV. endaimonia. contains the word daimwn in composition. XXII. The text is corrupt, but the words "or if it be but few" should be "that is little enough."

XXIII. "Plato": Republic, vi. p. 486 A.

XXV. "It will," etc. Euripides, Belerophon, frag. 287 (Nauck).

"Lives," etc. Euripides, Hypsipyle, frag. 757 (Nauck). "As long," etc. Aristophanes, Acharne, 66 i.

"Plato" Apology, p. 28 B.

"For thus" Apology, p. 28 F.

XXVI. "But, O noble sir," etc. Plato, Gorgias, 512 D.
XXVII. "And as for those parts," etc. A quotation from Euripides, Chryssipus, frag. 839 (Nauck).

"With meats," etc. From Euripides, Supplices, 1110.
XXXIII. "They both," i.e. life and wrestling.

"Says he" (63): Plato, quoted by Epictetus, Arr. i. 28, 2 and 22.

XXXVII. "How know we," etc. The Greek means: "how know we whether Telauges were not nobler in character than Sophocles?" The allusion is unknown.

XXVII. "Frost" The word is written by Casaubon as a proper name, "Pagus.'

"The hardihood of Socrates was famous"; see Plato, Siymposium, p. 220.

BOOK X XXII. The Greek means, "paltry breath bearing up corpses, so that the tale of Dead Man's Land is clearer."

XXII. "The poet" (21): Euripides, frag. 898 (Nauck); compare Aeschylus, Danaides, frag. 44.

XXIV. "Plato" (23): Theaetetus, p. 174 D.

XXXIV. "The poet" (34): Homer, Iliad, vi. 147.

XXXIV. "Wood": A translation of ulh, "matter."

XXXVIII. "Rhetoric" (38): Rather "the gift of speech"; or perhaps the "decree" of the reasoning faculty.

BOOK XI V. "Cithaeron" (6): Oedipus utters this cry after discovering that he has fulfilled his awful doom, he was exposed on Cithaeron as an infant to die, and the cry implies that he wishes he had died there. Sophocles, Oedipus Tyrannus, 1391.

V. "New Comedy...," etc. C. has here strayed from the Greek rather widely. Translate: "and understand to what end the New Comedy was adopted, which by small degrees degenerated into a mere show of skill in mimicry." C. writes Comedia Vetus, Media, Nova. XII. "Phocion" (13): When about to be put to death he charged his son to bear no malice against the Athenians.

XXVIII. "My heart," etc. (31): From Homer, Odyssey ix. 413. "They will" From Hesiod, Opera et Dies, 184.

"Epictetus" Arr. i. II, 37.

XXX. "Cut down grapes" (35): Correct "ears of corn." "Epictetus"(36): Arr. 3, 22, 105.

GLOSSARY

This Glossary includes all proper names (excepting a few which are insignificant or unknown) and all obsolete or obscure words. ADRIANUS, or Hadrian (76-138 A. D.), 14th Roman Emperor.

Agrippa, M. Vipsanius (63-12 B.C.), a distinguished soldier under Augustus.

Alexander the Great, King of Macedonia, and Conqueror of the East, 356-323 B.C.

Antisthenes of Athens, founder of the sect of Cynic philosophers, and an opponent of Plato, 5th century B.C Antoninus Pius, 15th Roman Emperor, 138-161 AD. one of the best princes that ever mounted a throne.

Apathia: the Stoic ideal was calmness in all circumstance an insensibility to pain, and absence of all exaltation at, pleasure or good fortune.

Apelles, a famous painter of antiquity.

Apollonius of Alexandria, called Dyscolus, or the 'ill-tempered,' a great grammarian.

Aposteme, tumour, excrescence.

Meditations

Archimedes of Syracuse 287-212 B.C., the most famous mathematician of antiquity.

Athos, a mountain promontory at the N. of the Aegean Sea.

Augustus, first Roman Emperor (ruled 31 B.C.-14 AD.).

Avoid, void.

BACCHIUS: there Were several persons of this name, and the one meant is perhaps the musician.

Brutus (1) the liberator of the Roman people from their kings, and (2) the murderer of Cæsar.

Both names were household words.

Cæsar, Caius, Julius, the Dictator and Conqueror.

Caieta, a town in Latium.

Camillus, a famous dictator in the early days of the Roman Republic.

Carnuntum, a town on the Danube in Upper Pannonia.

Cato, called of Utica, a Stoic who died by his own hand after the battle of Thapsus, 46 B.C. His name was proverbial for virtue and courage.

Cautelous, cautious.

Cecrops, first legendary King of Athens.

Charax, perhaps the priestly historian of that name, whose date is unknown, except that it must be later than Nero.

Chirurgeon, surgeon.

Chrysippus, 280-207 B.C., a Stoic philosopher, and the founder of Stoicism as a systematic philosophy.

Circus, the Circus Maximus at Rome, where games were held. There were four companies who contracted to provide horses, drivers, etc. These were called Factiones, and each had its distinguishing colour: russata (red), albata (white), veneta (blue), prasina (green). There was high rivalry between them, and riots and bloodshed not infrequently.

Cithaeron, a mountain range N. of Attica.

Comedy, ancient; a term applied to the Attic comedy of Aristophanes and his time, which criticised persons and politics, like a modern comic journal, such as Punck. See New Comedy.

Compendious, short.

Conceit, opinion.

Contentation, contentment.

Crates, a Cynic philosopher of the 4th century B.C.

Crœsus, King of Lydia, proverbial for wealth; he reigned 560-546 B.C.

Cynics, a school of philosophers, founded by Antisthenes. Their texts were a kind of caricature of Socraticism. Nothing was good but virtue, nothing bad but vice. The Cynics repudiated all civil and social claims, and attempted to return to what they called a state of nature. Many of them were very disgusting in their manners.

DEMETRIUS of Phalerum, an Athenian orator, statesman, philosopher, and poet. Born 345 B.C.

Democritus of Abdera (460-361 B.C.), celebrated as the 'laughing philosopher,' whose constant thought was 'What fools these mortals be.' He invented the Atomic Theory.

Dio of Syracuse, a disciple of Plato, and afterwards tyrant of Syracuse. Murdered 353 B.C.

Diogenes, the Cynic, born about 412 B.C., renowned for his rudeness and hardihood.

Diognetus, a painter.

Dispense with, put up with.

Dogmata, pithy sayings, or philosophical rules of life.

EMPEDOCLES of Agrigentum, fl. 5th century B.C., a philosopher, who first laid down that there were "four elements." He believed in the transmigration of souls, and the indestructibility of matter.

Epictetus, a famous Stoic philosopher. He was of Phrygia, at first a slave, then freedman, lame, poor, and contented. The work called Encheiridion was compiled by a pupil from his discourses.

Epicureans, a sect of philosophers founded by Epicurus, who "combined the physics of Democritus," i.e. the atomic theory, "with the ethics of Aristippus."

They proposed to live for happiness, but the word did not bear that coarse and vulgar sense originally which it soon took.

Epicurus of Samos, 342-270 B.C.

Lived at Athens in his "gardens," an urbane and kindly, if somewhat useless, life. His character was simple and temperate, and had none of the vice or indulgence which was afterwards associated with the name of Epicurean.

Eudoxus of Cnidus, a famous astronomer and physician of the 4th century B. C.

FATAL, fated.

Fortuit, chance (adj.).

Fronto, M. Cornelius, a rhetorician and pleader, made consul in 143 A.D. A number of his letters to M, Aur. and others are extant.

GRANUA, a tributary of the Danube.

HELICE, ancient capital city of Achaia, swallowed up by an earthquake, 373 B.C.

Helvidius Priscus, son-in-law of Thrasea Paetus, a noble man and a lover of liberty. He was banished by Nero, and put to death by Vespasian.

Heraclitus of Ephesus, who lived in the 6th century B.C. He wrote on philosophy and natural science.

Herculaneum, near Mount Vesuvius, buried by the eruption of 79 AD.

Hercules, p. 167, should be Apollo. See Muses.

Hiatus, gap.

Hipparchus of Bithynia, an astronomer of the 2nd century B.C., "The true father of astronomy."

Hippocrates of Cos, about 460-357 B.C. One of the most famous physicians of antiquity.

IDIOT, means merely the non-proficient in anything, the "layman," he who was not technically trained in any art, craft, or calling.

LEONNATUS, a distinguished general under Alexander the Great.

Lucilla, daughter of M. Aurelius, and wife of Verus, whom she survived.

MÆCENAS, a trusted adviser of Augustus, and a munificent patron of wits and literary men.

Maximus, Claudius, a Stoic philosopher.

Menippus, a Cynic philosopher.

Meteores, ta metewrologika, "high philosophy," used specially of astronomy and natural philosophy, which were bound up with other speculations.

Middle Comedy, something midway between the Old and New Comedy. See Comedy, Ancient, and New Comedy.

Middle things, Book 7, XXV. The Stoics divided all things into virtue, vice, and indifferent things; but as "indifferent" they regarded most of those things which the world regards as good or bad, such as wealth or poverty. Of these, some were "to be desired," some "to be rejected."

Muses, the nine deities who presided over various kinds of poesy, music, etc. Their leader was Apollo, one of whose titles is Musegetes, the Leader of the Muses.

NERVES, strings.

New Comedy, the Attic Comedy of Menander and his school, which criticised not persons but manners, like a modern comic opera. See Comedy, Ancient.

PALESTRA, wrestling school.

Pancratiast, competitor in the pancratium, a combined contest which comprised boxing and wrestling.

Parmularii, gladiators armed with a small round shield (parma).

Pheidias, the most famous sculptor of antiquity.

Philippus, founder of the Macedonian supremacy, and father of Alexander the Great.

Phocion, an Athenian general and statesman, a noble and high-minded man, 4th century B.C.

He was called by Demosthenes, "the pruner of my periods."

He was put to death by the State in 317, on a false suspicion, and left a message for his son "to bear no grudge against the Athenians."

Pine, torment.

Plato of Athens, 429-347 B.C. He used the dialectic method invented by his master Socrates.

He was, perhaps, as much poet as philosopher. He is generally identified with the Theory of Ideas, that things are what they are by participation with our eternal Idea. His "Commonwealth" was a kind of Utopia.

Platonics, followers of Plato.

Pompeii, near Mount Vesuvius, buried in the eruption of 79 A. D.

Pompeius, C. Pompeius Magnus, a very successful general at the end of the Roman Republic (106-48 B.C.).

Prestidigitator, juggler.

Pythagoras of Samos, a philosopher, scientist, and moralist of the 6th century B.C.

QUADI, a tribe of S. Germany.

M. Aurelius carried on war against them, and part of this book was written in the field.

RICTUS, gape, jaws.

Rusticus, Q. Junius, or Stoic philosopher, twice made consul by M. Aurelius.

SACRARY, shrine.

Salaminius, Book 7, XXXVII. Leon of Sala-mis. Socrates was ordered by the Thirty Tyrants to fetch him before them, and Socrates, at his own peril, refused.

Sarmatae, a tribe dwelling in Poland.

Sceletum, skeleton.

Sceptics, a school of philosophy founded by Pyrrho (4th century B.C.). He advocated "suspension of judgment," and taught the relativity of knowledge and impossibility of proof. The school is not unlike the Agnostic school.

Scipio, the name of two great soldiers, P. Corn. Scipio Africanus, conqueror of Hannibal, and P.

Corn. Sc. Afr. Minor, who came into the family by adoption, who destroyed Carthage.

Secutoriani (a word coined by C.), the Sececutores, light-armed gladiators, who were pitted against others with net and trident.

Sextus of Chaeronea, a Stoic philosopher, nephew of Plutarch.

Silly, simple, common.

Sinuessa, a town in Latium.

Socrates, an Athenian philosopher (469-399 B.C.), founder of the dialectic method. Put to death on a trumped-up charge by his countrymen.

Stint, limit (without implying niggardliness).

Meditations

Stoics, a philosophic system founded by Zeno (4th century B.C.), and systematised by Chrysippus (3rd century B.C.). Their physical theory was a pantheistic materialism, their summum bonum "to live according to nature." Their wise man needs nothing, he is sufficient to himself; virtue is good, vice bad, external things indifferent.

THEOPHRASTUS, a philosopher, pupil of Aristotle, and his successor as president of the Lyceum. He wrote a large number of works on philosophy and natural history. Died 287 B.C.

Thrasea, P. Thrasea Pactus, a senator and Stoic philosopher, a noble and courageous man. He was condemned to death by Nero.

Tiberius, 2nd Roman Emperor (14-31 AD.). He spent the latter part of his life at Capreae (Capri), off Naples, in luxury or debauchery, neglecting his imperial duties.

To-torn, torn to pieces.

Trajan, 13th Roman Emperor, 52-117 A.D.

VERUS, Lucius Aurelius, colleague of M. Aurelius in the Empire.

He married Lucilla, daughter of M. A., and died 169 A.D.

Vespasian, 9th Roman Emperor XENOCRATES of Chalcedon, 396-314 B.C., a philosopher, and president of the Academy.

Printed in Great Britain
by Amazon

ce5cb6b6-33a5-498c-b79c-39189aaa92d0R03